The Way of the Sun Dragon

Chinese Martial Art of Tai-Yang Lung Tao

by
Kenneth A. Smith

Asian Humanities Press
Berkeley, California

ASIAN HUMANITIES PRESS

Asian Humanities Press offers to the specialist and the general reader alike, the best in new translations of major works and significant original contributions, to enhance our understanding of Asian literature, religions, cultures and thought.

Library of Congress Cataloging-in-Publication Data

Smith, Kenneth A., 1956-
    The way of the sun dragon: Chinese martial art of tai-yang lung tao / by Kenneth A. Smith.
        p.   cm.
    ISBN 0-87573-026-4
    1. Martial arts—China. 2. Taoism. I. Title.
GV1100.7.A2S65   1993
796.8'0951—dc20   92-31468
                                                          CIP

Contents

Introduction

A few words of introduction are necessary concerning the study and scope of this manual. Although much of the material presented on these pages may seem rather simplistic, it is not intended for casual investigation only. This is a serious "*workbook*." It was written to be studied over the course of a lifetime. This information should be read and reread, again and again, thoroughly pondered and contemplated, tried and tested.

One cannot judge *Tai-Yang Lung Tao* from its appearance alone. To try to understand the complexity hidden within the simplicity of the art by merely observing its outer movements is like attempting to explore the depths of the ocean from atop a mountain. To truly understand life in the water, one must get wet. We are sorry, but there simply are no magical shortcuts to this type of comprehension.

Yet, the key which unlocks the doors of enlightenment has not been hidden from you. The only secret in all of the martial arts is that *there are no secrets*. All knowledge and skill lies somewhere within you, waiting to be released into your conscious mind and made manifest in your life. This is accomplished through education–from the latin *educere* which means to bring out, like you would bring water out of a well. But, the only type of education which truly exists is "self-education," obtained through good old-fashioned hard work.

If you do not make progress quickly, however, you must not blame the teacher, because the teacher cannot magically confer his/her knowledge and skills upon you. You must internalize all the information given and correlate it with that which you draw up from deep within yourself. Learning cannot be made compulsory or forced upon you in any way. Either you wish to remember the information, guided by your teacher's promptings, or you do not.

This is one major way in which the Way of the Sun Dragon differs from all other martial arts. We do not assume that the potential student knows nothing and we are going to "teach" it all to him/her in bits and pieces. Quite the contrary. We begin with the premise that the potential student already knows all there is to know, and the "teacher" is merely there to remind him/her that he/she knows it. Learning is no longer an attempt to collect knowledge, but a process of recalling that which is a natural part of one's own being.

This book, therefore, represents the study of the martial arts, not merely as a means of self-defense but as a living "*experience.*" Yet, life cannot be frozen upon the pages of a book for leisurely analysis. It is always dying and fading away, moment by moment, into the past. Although we are involved in it, right here and now, its vital essence seems to always remain just beyond our mental grasp. We strive, therefore, to reach into the source of Being and to comprehend the nature of Life. Any type of investigation, art or ritualized practice could be effectively used to serve this purpose. However, *Tai-Yang Lung Tao* includes such a broad spectrum of life, of what it is to be human, that it is well suited to this task. It provides us with a means of physical training and self-defense, coordination of the Lifeforce or internal energy, mental discipline, and spiritual philosophy. Our purpose of study should not be merely to become adept at fighting skills, even strictly for self-defense. It should be a total personal transformation that we seek, one that will manifest itself in every sphere of our life.

We will follow the methods of instruction used by the ancient Chinese, rather than those employed by the western world. In the Orient, the teacher does not pause to prove the theories or philosophies which he/she is presenting to the students. Nor does he/she argue with the class or invite debate. Instead, the teacher proceeds to deliver the lesson exactly as it was given to him/her, without waiting to see if they are all in agreement. It is not important whether the teachings are accepted as truth or not. Those who are ready for such truth will instinctively know it when they hear it. As for all others, if they are determined to deny reality, no amount of facts and/or argument will ever convince them. The teacher knows, however, that truth is a seed which often sprouts and grows only with the passage of time.

We do not infer that the student should accept every truth which is presented to him/her. Quite the contrary. Everything that is written upon these pages, or given to them by a teacher, may just be a lie or a pale fantasy. No truth is a truth if it cannot be proven to oneself through experience. Therefore, accept nothing without proof. But, if you are wise, you will be guided by the advice of those who have travelled the path ahead of you.

In choosing the information to include in this manual, we were forced to decide whether to focus upon theory–history, ethics, philosophy, universal principles, etc.–or to concentrate more specifically upon the practice of *Tai-Yang Lung Tao*–techniques, exercises, strategies, etc. We settled, finally, upon a compromise and compiled a basic treatise that would deal with all aspects of this rare art.

We did not use photographs to illustrate the postures in this book because we felt that students should learn to reproduce the pure essence of each posture or movement, not merely imitate a particular person's variation of that essence. It is important for the practitioner to discover his/her own expression of the universal principles of *Tai-Yang Lung Tao*.

Do not ever become discouraged with your performance, however, no matter how crude it may seem to you. No one can perform the postures and forms of this art perfectly, because perfection is a relative thing, an ideal dependent upon one's individual perception. It is, therefore, a constantly evolving dynamic, since our perception of the universe is constantly evolving and expanding. Perfection is a never-ending journey, not a destination.

The meditations, physical disciplines and rituals described in this book are merely some of the tools which the student may use to reawaken to the power within him/herself. Please, feel free to adopt and adapt any or all of the material which you find here to suit your own "inner quest" for the Self.

As with any other type of physical activity, consult with your physician and get a picture of your state of health, as well as his/her approval, before embarking on any major change in your present lifestyle.

HISTORICAL BACKGROUND

Tracing the origin of any martial art would be a difficult, if not outright impossible, task. Furthermore, the trail is almost entirely obscured by the fact that most martial arts are not the product of a single mind, but the evolution of a few core concepts, passed on from teacher to student over countless generations. And, in China, these core concepts were usually drawn from the prevalent *Buddhist/Taoist* traditions, reaching back into history several thousand years, at least. It has only been within the last six or seven centuries, however, that these traditions have evolved into the many Chinese martial systems known today as *Kung-Fu*.

It was in the year of the Dragon (1736 AD) that a boy was born in a nameless village in the northern provinces of China, a boy who would one day become the founder of a most unusual style of martial arts. His name was *Fong Su-Yi*.

When he was but nine years old, the soldiers of the *Manchu* emperor invaded his village. Many of his friends, their families and his own relatives were murdered and their homes burned as the usurpers sought out and executed all patriots and loyal followers of the fallen *Ming* emperor (1644 AD). Those who were not put to death were robbed of their possessions and publicly humiliated.

Fearing for their son's life, his parents sent *Fong Su-Yi* to the ancient monastery upon the slopes of *Shao-Shih*, near humble *Teng-Fon-Hsien* in *Honan* province. For many years he was, literally, kept a prisoner within the monastery walls, receiving no further word of the civil war which raged outside or the fate of his parents. Eventually, he became accustom to the routine of monastic life, performing his assigned duties without complaint. The monks educated him upon the teachings of the Buddha and the mystical *Tao* of Lao-Tsu. And, through one of the elder monks, *Su-Yi* discovered the complex symbology of the *I-Ching*, the ancient "Book of Change." This aged mentor also taught him the subtle principles of meditation and several styles of martial arts. But, he still ached for news of home.

So, early in the year of the Rabbit (1759 AD), *Fong Su-Yi* escaped from the monastery and returned to his village. He found his home burned to the ground and two crude grave markers grimly standing beneath a tree a short distance away. His parents were gone, and so was his past.

His heart empty, *Fong Su-Yi* turned back toward the security of the monastery, where he would seclude himself from the world outside. Unknown to him, however, the brotherhood had provided refuge to many of the *Ming* family and their loyal servants. The *Ching* emperor, whom the *Manchu* had placed upon the royal throne, had learned of this treason through his vast network of spies and sent an army to destroy the temple. *Shaolin* was in flames and its monks either dead or scattered by the time that *Fong Su-Yi* arrived again in the year of the Dragon (1760 AD).

Fong Su-Yi wandered aimlessly across the countryside for many years, living as a beggar and fighting the *Manchu* at every opportunity. But, with each passing year, the anger grew in his gut like a cancer, devouring him, until he could no longer bear to watch his people being treated like animals. So, with only a few meager provisions and his most cherished possession, a worn and tattered copy of the *I-Ching* given to him by his aged mentor, he turned his steps to the northeast until he came to the peninsula of *Korea* and the village of *Kumhwa*. There he remained.

For several years he worked as an apprentice to the local blacksmith, filling his days with sweat and labor but his nights with meditation and study. He spent every evening exploring and contemplating the vast complexities of the elusive *I-Ching*. It was from this esoteric influence that his unique martial arts philosophies evolved into the art of *Tai-Yang Lung Tao*, the Way of the Sun Dragon.

In the spring of the year of the Ram (1775AD) *Fong Su-Yi* left the forge and, with only his crumbling copy of the *I-Ching*, journeyed alone into the mountains west of the village. He did not return to *Kumhwa* until the first snows began to fall. But, he did not return as a blacksmith. His skin was no longer smudged with ash and smoke, although a mysterious fire did seem to burn in his eyes as he spoke to everyone who would listen about the simplicity which he had discovered hidden within the numerous complexities of the martial arts.

Over the remainder of his life, until his death in the year of the Dragon (1820 AD) at the age of 84, *Fong Su-Yi* continued to refine and develop his perception of these universal principles into his own system of martial arts. Borrowing heavily from Taoist folklore, he created his own cosmological mythology linked to the numerological symbology of the *I-Ching* and translated this into a ritualized physical practice. He named this art "the Way of the Sun Dragon," or *Tai-Yang Lung Tao*.

ORIGINS OF THE SUN DRAGON

All matter in the endless universe is merely a form of *vibration*, energy particles slowed down, the essence of light made visible. This is basic physics. All things are merely different manifestations of one universal "*Source.*" Everything fits in somewhere on the vibratory rate scale. At the lower end of the spectrum, with the slowest rate of vibration, is solid physical matter. Next is sound, with a slightly faster rate of vibration, and then heat, light and even thought.

Within each classification are also slight variations of the basic vibratory rate. Those vibrations of matter which fall within the range of soundwaves may be further subdivided into lower tones, which move in longer and slower waves, or higher tones, which move in shorter and faster wave patterns. The higher vibrations of matter that are interpreted as lightwaves may be divided into reds, which move slowest, at one end of the visible spectrum and blues, which move fastest, at the other end.

Nothing is truly independent of anything else. The entire universe is interconnected by a single common denominator–the essence of vibration. As a result, we have direct control over our environment through the vibrations of our thought, if we will simply acknowledge and accept responsibility for our every action and thought.

It is, therefore, possible to taste sound, hear odors, and feel color. Even the mundane occurrences of our daily lives can become spiritually enlightening experiences, if we but open up our minds to the entire spectrum of Life. Anything spiritual has to have a physical reality as its base, simply attached at the opposite end of the vibratory spectrum.

According to the ancient *Taoist* story of the creation of the universe, before anything else existed there was only the dark emptiness of the *Void*, known in Chinese as *Wu-Chi*. The mysterious something that first originated from out of this Nothingness is known as *Tai-Chi*, or the Grand Ultimate, and is symbolized by a uniquely simple diagram. (See illustration Figure A.)

Liang-Yi, or the Two Forms, represented by the colors black and white, manifested in the Great Emptiness as the twin polarities of *Yin-Yang*, the negative and the positive, the female and the male, all opposites in a perfect state of balance. But, even though these antithetical forces seem to stand against each other in nature, they are also quite inseparable. This can be seen by the small speck of each which appears in the heart of the other. They are in such perfect balance that one is always giving birth to the other. Extreme *Yin* is the beginning of *Yang*, and extreme *Yang* is the beginning of *Yin*. For example, when the sun is at its apex, at noon or thereabouts, it is the beginning of sunset.

The two polarities, then, gave birth to the Four Symbols, or *Su-Hsiang*. These four are the essences of Earth or *Greater Yin*, Water or *Lesser Yin*, Fire or *Lesser Yang* and Air or *Greater Yang*. But, these are not necessarily the literal elements. They are, instead, merely symbols for the four classifications of matter as it appears in the physical universe. *Air* is symbolic of all matter in its gaseous state, as it gathered together in the infinite Void. *Fire* is the energy-releasing state between matter and pure force, a result of the explosive interaction of these first molecular clouds. *Water* is symbolic of all matter in its liquid state, condensed in the furnace of the Big Bang. *Earth* is symbolic of all matter in its solid state, congealed during the cooling of the new universe.

These four elements, finally, came together and interacted in endless combinations to create the *Ten Thousand*

Things. This is the poetic way of the ancient *Taoist* to describe the vast array of physical manifestations in the universe.

However, this simple tale of creation seems, somehow, far too impersonal and a bit too logical to the mind of the average superstitious person. Do not, though, leap to any hasty conclusions concerning the use of the word "*superstitious.*" We are all superstitious in our need to personify forces that are beyond our present ability to fully comprehend. And, there is nothing at all wrong in that, if it is a positive imagery and helps us to better relate to such forces.

From the dawn of Humanity's short existence upon this isolated little world, he/she has personified the "*Source of All*" and Its infinite manifestations in any number of ways. Whether it is by the name of *Giche Manitou* (the Great Spirit) of the Amerindian, or *Zeus* upon Mount Olympus, or *Jehovah*, or *Yaweh*, or simply as *God*, all are but different names for the same "*First Cause of Everything.*" Each is merely a different expression of individual understanding. We shall leave the futile argument of whether the *Absolute* is a *Divine Being* or an abstract "*Force*" to those who thrive on such trivialities. It is enough to know that the One simply "*IS.*"

A genderless "*Force*" so far beyond our intelligence's ability to grasp that we have only a vague understanding of its existence, seems untouchable to most. Yet, we still wish to communicate with It. Through the vehicle of a symbolic representation, a microscopic model of the macrocosm, this is possible.

Among the first symbols for the *Absolute*, and one which lingers even into the present day, is the blazing orb of the *sun*, known in Chinese as *Tai-Yang*. It is the Giver of Life and our planet would not long survive without its light. Even on the darkest of nights, its light is still with us, reflected from the silver face of its child, the moon. Its light even burns deep within our own physical bodies, metaphorically. Thus, we have the "*solar*" plexus.

Fong Su-Yi chose the dynamic symbol of the sun to represent the radiant source of all creation, *Tai-Chi*, the Grand Ultimate. From this One, he imagined the great two-headed Dragon of the *Yin-Yang* emerging to become the instrument of creation. This magnificent Beast of Heaven is known in Chinese as *Tai-Yang Lung*, the Sun Dragon. Its living breath became the Four Essences, which were transformed by the Divine Force of its thought into the *Pa-Kua*, the Eight Qualities of reality as expressed in the Eight Trigrams of the *I-Ching*, the Book of Changes.

The *I-Ching* is the oldest known book in the entire world, dating back more than three thousand years to the *Hsia Dynasty* (2205-1766 BC). And, although it has been widely used as a tool of divination, it is not a method of "fortune telling." Nor is it a religious book, but a collection of symbolic wisdom that explains the complexity of the universe in terms of simple numerical equations and philosophical correlations. It is not intended to "predict" the future, merely to serve as an aid to comprehending the ever-changing phenomena of the universe.

Emperor Fu-Hsi, the legendary founder of the first dynasty (2205 BC), is the purported creator of the *I-Ching*. It is said that the great Dragon of Heaven disclosed to him the invisible *Threads of Change* from which the fabric of the universe was woven, and revealed to him the paradoxical nature of *Yin-Yang* in the form of broken and solid lines etched into the rock of the Earth. *Fu-Hsi*, then, arranged these lines into the *Pa-Kua*, the Eight Trigrams symbolic of the elemental forces of nature created by the influence of *Yin-Yang* on the *Su-Hsiang*, the Four Symbols.

GREATER YANG	LESSER YANG	LESSER YIN	GREATER YIN
(air)	(fire)	(water)	(earth)

These four elemental essences, then, represented all of the possible combinations of *Yin* and *Yang* upon each other. But, since the universe was created by a trinity of forces (electrons, protons and neutrons), *Fu-Hsi* added a third line to this basic formation and discovered the eight quintessential forces of the natural world, which are symbolized by the *Pa-Kua*.

1. ___ ___
   ___ ___   KUN (earth)
   ___ ___   receptive, dark, nourishing

2. _____
   ___ ___   KEN (mountain)
   ___ ___   stillness, tranquility, stubbornness

3. ___ ___
   _____   KHAN (water)
   ___ ___   deep, dangerous, difficult

4. _____
   _____   SUN (wind)
   ___ ___   piercing, honest, simple

5. _____
   _____   TIEN (heaven)
   _____   creative, strong, light

6. ___ ___
   _____   TUI (marsh)
   _____   open, excessive, pleasure

7. _____
   ___ ___   LI (fire)
   _____   clarity, dependent, conscious

8. ___ ___
   ___ ___   CHEN (thunder)
   _____   arousing, growth, expansive

These are the only eight possible combinations of the three *Yin-Yang* lines (2x2x2=8). Beyond their fundamental imagery, further meaning may be inferred through the inter-relationship of the *Kua* symbologies of season, time of day, family members, and so forth. The *Pa-Kua* do not represent these elements themselves but their tendencies in movement and form. For this reason, they are most commonly seen arranged in a progressive circle of creation and destruction. Their positions on this circle reflect their opposition to each other. (See illustration Figure B.)

Fu-Hsi discovered that when the trigrams were placed one atop another, again symbolizing the relationship of *Yin-Yang*, the result was sixty-four hexagrams (8x8=64). And, like the *Pa-Kua*, these hexagrams were a combination of strong solid lines and/or yielding broken lines, creating a specific pattern of energy flow, much like that of a modern electrical circuit.

In point of fact, it was this *Fu-Hsi* arrangement which led the seventeenth century mathematician Gottfried Wilhelm Leibniz to the discovery of a functioning binary system. Without this major revelation, our world would be a much more primitive place today, since this binary code discovered by Leibniz became the basis of all computer functions and languages.

A Jesuit priest returning from China, Father Joachim Bouvet, showed the ancient *Fu-Hsi* arrangement to Leibniz. The Father of Modern Calculus was amazed to find that if he substituted a zero for each broken line and a one for each solid line, then read the hexagram from bottom to top as the Chinese did, in the order assigned to them by *Fu-Hsi*, he got the series 000000, 000001, 000010, 000011, 000100, 000101, 000110, 000111, and so forth. This proved to be the binary notations for the numbers zero to sixty-three, inclusive and conclusive.

Each hexagram of the *I-Ching* may be thought of, therefore, as a kind of energy circuit, composed of open switches or broken lines and closed switches or solid lines. Each specific energy pattern represents a different aspect of the universal flow of life-force energy as it is channelled through the common threads of our existence.

Since this power of the number two (0/1 or *Yin-Yang*) manifests in all natural structures, modern scholars and scientists have been able to apply the abstract mathematical principles of the *I-Ching* to nearly everything from simple crystalline formations to DNA, even to the movements of the galaxies themselves. The ancient Chinese oracle of the *I-Ching* is, therefore, a direct representation of Albert Einstein's famous Theory of Relativity. It is a method of exploring the intimate relationship which exists between the observer and the reality manifest in the observation.

Perhaps in some future publication we shall expound more completely upon the intricacies of this original *I-Ching* of *Fu-Hsi*, but it is enough for now that you understand something of the philosophical background from which *Fong Su-Yi* extracted his unique view of the universe and the martial arts.

A MATTER OF ETHICS

It is an obvious fact that life does not often conform to our ideals or our philosophies. We would all like the world to be a utopia of beauty and peace, but it is just as often an ugly and violent place in which to live. As humans, we must not turn our backs to the reality of the negative side of life in order to focus upon the positive. We must often be warriors of peace.

Among the people of this world, there is no such thing as a true pacifist, a being with no aggression. Each and every one of us has violence in his/her emotional and mental nature, whether it is the outward violence of an actual physical assault or the inner violence of silent anger. What marks the difference between the barbarian and the civilized person, however, is the threshold at which this violence comes forth. For the former, all it may take is a single word of insult or even an aggressive look. But, for the latter, it requires a life-or-death situation from which there is no possible escape.

Violence is within each and every one of us, whether we believe it or not. So, what are we to do about it? There are some who think that it is best to just ignore it and pray that it goes away by itself. Others preach against it and declare it to be the "work of the devil," vainly attempting to suppress it and bury it deep in their souls. These foolish people, by thrusting a cap down upon their emotions, are like volcanoes waiting to erupt into even worse violence.

To truly know peace, one must also know violence. But, violence does not necessarily need to be destructive. And, likewise, peace is not always a force for good.

By not physically defending yourself, by trying to be a man/woman of peace and allowing your assailant to have his/her way with you, you harm this person more than if you had actually struck back. Not only does he/she remain ignorant of the error of such violence, but he/she will probably go on to commit the same error against someone else. The evil of his/her actions will continue to grow because you were too selfish to risk a compromise of your morality in order to teach this person a much needed lesson.

But, if you had only applied the same strict code to your personal defense and showed your assailant that the error of such actions could lead to his/her own destruction (without actually destroying the person), you could have rescued him/her from the Law of *Retribution*, the cosmic cycle of Cause and Effect which will one day bring the evil of his/her actions back to its point of origin. By taking no action, though, you have helped him/her to spread this evil in the world. On the other hand, if you were to use too much violence while defending yourself, you would still be adding to the evil in the world through your own actions.

Your path, once you have found it, therefore, will lead you through the realm of *Neutrality*. You will follow neither the right nor the left path, the positive nor the negative, yet you will manifest both of these qualities at the same time. You will follow no particular philosophy or artificial code of morality created by Man/Woman. Your feet will remain upon the center path of Neutrality.

The art of *Tai-Yang Lung Tao* is comprised of principles and techniques which will allow its practitioners to evolve to a higher state of control over the animalistic side of their own personalities. It teaches the student not to force these changes but to gently guide his/her mind and emotions along a preset path to enlightenment, without being self-critical or judgemental.

The first step onto the path takes place when one realizes that there is a need to refine the quality of the inner self.

By the time that this awareness has unfolded, the person has already passed through the first two levels of spiritual development and is firmly planted upon the third level. From here, then, the student seeks out a teacher to set his/her feet upon the correct path into the fourth level and beyond.

Only human beings may sink below the level of the beasts of the jungle, and this is the realm of the first level of physical reaction. A being enmeshed in this world of emotional insanity will attack and kill another person for no reason at all, other than the warped sense of excitement and power that the kill gives him/her.

The second level of physical reaction harbors beings of only slightly more rationality, but it is still a distorted kind of logic which motivates such actions. Here, a being will provoke a violent response from an innocent victim, so that he/she may feel justified for destroying this person. Because they did not throw the "first punch," they will pronounce their actions, no matter how unnecessarily violent, to have been in self-defense. They have developed only enough human rationality to understand what will drive another person into a violent reaction.

The third level of response, unfortunately, is the most heavily populated. It is the realm of perhaps eighty to ninety percent of all mankind. Here, a person will neither attack nor provoke an attack from another person. But, should such a person be physically assaulted him/herself, they will react with as much thoughtless violence as they are capable of producing to either cripple or kill their assailant.

It is the fourth level, however, that all martial artists should strive to achieve. Upon this plane of mental and emotional existence a being will, also, neither attack nor provoke an attack. But, unlike others of his/her kind, if such a person were to be physically assaulted, they would respond in such a way as to defend themselves yet do the least amount of harm possible to their opponent. Such a being has learned the importance of *mercy*. This does not, albeit, mean that such a person is incapable of doing severe damage. Under the proper circumstances, such a reaction could be necessary to preserve life, either their own or that of a loved one, but this would be viewed as a last resort only.

There is a fifth level of reaction, rarely seen in this world of violence. A person who has achieved this mystical level would treat any form of attack, vocal or physical or psychic, as if it were so many flower petals being scattered at his/her feet. Such a person would not win a thousand wars by fighting a thousand battles, but would win by not fighting at all. Such a person has entered a state known as *Wu-Ti*, meaning literally "no enemy - no rival." He/she strives never to contend but, if a conflict should arise, harbors no animosity toward the opponent.

Any event or circumstance which draws you into a state of mental or emotional imbalance must be immediately neutralized and corrected. But, to merely neutralize an antagonist's physical actions, without resolving his/her emotional motivations, will not regain balance and harmony. The real imbalancing influence is still active and must be dealt with accordingly.

Do not, however, leap to any misconception that this allows you to do as you wish and rationalize it away through the tenets of any religion or convenient philosophy. Be assured that the Law of Retribution, known in the Orient as *Karma*, will catch up to you just as it will to your assailant.

Whenever possible, help those less fortunate than yourself to learn their lessons in life. But, this does not mean that you should interfere with their chosen course. Help can take the form of offered advice, shown compassion, or merely acting as an example through your own experiences. Do not seek to take charge of anyone's life, except your own, but do not turn your back on anyone either. If you can give assistance, give it freely and with joy.

PRINCIPLES OF KUNG-FU

For some unknown reason, there is still a trend in this country, even among seasoned practitioners, to classify all forms of martial arts under the generic titles of either *Karate* or *Kung-Fu*. This would be the same as grouping violins and trumpets into the same section of the orchestra, simply because they both produce music. One belongs to the string section and the other to the brass section. And, in neither of these sections would you find the drums or the keyboard instruments. So, too, are there literally hundreds of martial arts which do not belong to either classification of *Karate* or *Kung-Fu*, although their basic techniques and practices may seem quite similar.

In point of fact, *Kung-Fu* is not technically a martial arts classification at all. The actual Chinese term for the study of the martial arts is *Wu-Shu*. *Kung-Fu* is more of a fundamental philosophy which should underscore all disciplines, martial or otherwise. This becomes even more obvious when we translate this terminology into English. *Kung* (effort/energy expended) and *Fu* (time spent) refer to the dedication and effort of time required in the mastery of any physical skill. For example: if there were a secretary in an office building who was thoroughly and firmly convinced that he/she were fully capable of typing at a rate of two thousand words per minute and he/she spent many years in concentrated effort toward the achievement of this goal, he/she would be *Kung-Fu* in the skill of typing–upon successful completion of this quest.

Because of the vast diversity of this complex philosophy of *Kung-Fu*, no single book could ever hope to touch upon more than the most rudimentary manifestations of its physical principles within the martial arts. This book will, therefore, merely focus upon and introduce the student to the basic and intermediate levels of skills and practices of *Tai-Yang Lung Tao*, the Way of the Sun Dragon. These principles are not unique to the art of *Fon Su-Yi*, however. They are universal to all disciplines and philosophies, mainly because they are nothing more than logic and common sense.

Begin by knowing that you are the center of the universe. Your awareness radiates outward in all directions, beholding Infinity at every turn. Above and below, before and behind, left and right, inside and outside, never more and never less, there is always *Infinity*. And, any single point that is equidistant from all its boundaries is the center of the structure. But, since the universe is limitless, its structure has an infinite number of centers. This may seem like an impossible paradox of geometry. However, it is a logical reality. Each individual is, therefore, the absolute center of the universe as he/she sees it.

This center of the universe may be thought of as a micro-pipeline through which the infinite energies of the macrocosm flow. This vital force, or *Ming*, is channeled through the dense physical self along a pathway roughly corresponding to the spinal cord. It is, then, divided into its various forms as it is focused through three valve-like centers known as the *San-Ho* (the Three Rivers). These "valves" and the "pipeline" are intimately interconnected with the brain and its central nervous system, controlling the amount and type of life-force that courses through the physical body. (See illustration Figure C.)

Your daily intake of food, water and air is magically transmuted into several different types of quasi-electrical energies through complex biochemical reactions within the digestive system. This energy is circulated via conductive tissues throughout the entire organism. Every cell of the body, then, functions like a miniature storage battery, building up substantial charges of this bioelectrical energy. Collectively, these countless storage cells create a subtle electromagnetic field around the whole body. Under certain conditions, this fundamental life-force energy may interact with the oxygen molecules surrounding the physical form, ionizing them and creating a vague glow or aura effect. This process is known as *Lien Chi Hua Shen* (transmuting physical force to spirit), and may be quite easily seen by the untrained eye.

The life-force of *Ming*, as we have seen, is actually three separate energies acting as one. First, there is the "seed" force of the physical body known in Chinese as *Jing*, or as *Kundalini* in the sanskrit language of *Yoga*, emanating from the first "valve" at the base of the spine. Then, there is the "breath" force of the inner self known as *Chi*, or *Prana*, emanating from the solar plexus. This is the same energy manipulated by the acupuncturist and sought after by the martial artist. And, lastly, there is the "spirit" force known as *Shen*, or *Atma*, which emanates from the *Tien-Yen* (heaven's eye) at the center of the brow.

These three energies work together as the one life=force of *Ming* to animate the human being, both internally and externally. This is the primal substance of all life generated from *Wu-Chi*, the Great Emptiness, which courses through each and every cell of your body. It is Totality, the Mother/Father of All Things, spiralling around and through everything that is, was or ever shall be. It is the Trinity of forces which science would recognize as electron, proton and neutron. It is the infinitely diverse balance of energies known as *Tai-Chi*, the Grand Ultimate.

From the moment you were born until the moment you die, you have as much power at your disposal as you will ever have–*Infinity*. Simply open the three valves of the *San-Ho* and allow the life-force of the universe to flow through its center, you!

This center of your physical universe may be thought of as an invisible energy shell, or "silk cocoon" known as *Chan-Su* in Chinese. (See illustration Figure D.) Within this mystical bubble you feel safe and secure. Anything beyond its three foot diameter–give or take a few inches–is no real threat to you. It is only when an object, such as a fist, comes within its perimeter that there is a real danger. Therefore, do not be concerned with anything beyond the boundary of your cocoon.

As you journey through your life, many people and things will pass through this energy shell. Some will be welcome and feel comfortable, while others will make you uneasy and nervous the moment they enter your *field of presence*. Learn to listen to the silent voice of such feelings and trust in their primordial instincts. They are a vital part of you basic survival mechanism, and they will often tell you more about a person or a place than all of your other senses combined. In a world of violence and chaos, that could mean your life . . . or death.

Our modern "civilization" has, unfortunately, caused such instincts to become dormant. To reawaken and sharpen this subtle sensory awareness, you must learn to practice the forgotten art of pure observation, but not with your eyes alone. You must feel the relationship between the vibratory energies of your cocoon and those of your immediate environment. Do not, however, allow yourself to become too grim or serious in your observations.

Unfocus your attention, do not even think, and allow your mind to just float free and unhindered. Perceive everything around you at once and, unconsciously, evaluate your surroundings according to the symbology of the *Four Elements*.

Number one should always be the general mood of the place in which you find yourself. This rather vague quality is represented by the gaseous state of *Air*, and may be felt upon the surface of your energy shell like a warm or cold mist, depending upon the mental projections of the people present. Does it feel warm and friendly? Or, is it cold and threatening?

Number two would be an assessment of the temperature and available light, which are manifestations of the element of Fire. If it is too hot or too cold, your body will be drained of its strength very quickly. If there is insufficient light, you may not be able to see your assailant and will have to rely upon other senses to guide you. This may, however, be just as much of an advantage as it is a disadvantage. The absence of light will blind your opponent as much as it will you.

Number three is an awareness of atmospheric conditions, which is symbolized by the liquid element of *Water*. Each manifestation of weather (i.e. snow, rain, wind, etc.) may be either an aid or a hindrance to your defensive strategies. Wind may blow up debris into you face, blinding you, or you may put the wind to your back and allow the debris to work against your assailant. The same is true of rain. Deep snow may hinder escape or evasive footwork, or it may be kicked up into your opponent's face to distract him/her.

Number four would be almost any kind of physical obstacle, anything which might block your escape or your ability to defend yourself. These things belong to the element of *Earth*. A low doorway or a tree branch could make serious contact with your head. Tables, chairs, rocks, roots, or anything else underfoot could make you stumble into disaster. But, if you should find your avenues of escape cut off by such obstacles, it will also limit the number of opponents who can approach you at once. A cramped and cluttered space may be as much of a benefit as it is an annoyance.

Once you have successfully developed this habit of evaluating the safety of your immediate surroundings, you should turn you attention to the actual methods of self-defense, both internally through the understanding of your emotional responses and externally through the comprehension of physical dynamics.

All martial arts, no matter how different they may outwardly seem, are based upon the same four simple principles. All possible techniques, or combinations of techniques, are merely an application of one or more of the *Four Elements*. How one chooses to manifest these principles, however, will determine which martial art is being utilized.

The first, and most important, of these principles is that of *Perception* and *Prevention*, symbolized by the subtle element of *Air*. And, just as air is matter in a tenuous and gaseous state, Prevention is defense in its most refined form. It is epitomized by the logical actions of the intellect, applied through focused concentration, to recognize and neutralize any possible violence before it can take place.

The second, and most practical, form of physical defense is the principle of *Alignment* and *Evasion*, which is represented by the element of *Fire*. Simply stated, this means that the best defense is "*do not be there when the attack arrives*." In a street situation, this could spell the difference between life or death. And, it could be as simple as running away, or it could be exemplified, in the case of a competitor, by the bob and weave of a professional boxer. But, just as fire is matter in its energy-releasing state, Evasion is the release of physical energy from a perceptive state of consciousness. It is, in more technical terms, the motion of the observer into alignment with and away from the direct line of incoming force. This may be accomplished either horizontally (side-stepping or spinning) or vertically (leaping or dropping down).

The third principle, *Redirection* and *Projection*, is the most widely utilized aspect of the martial arts. It is uniquely symbolized by the element of *Water*, and it may manifest as a fluid throwing technique, projecting the force of the assailant down and away from the defender, or as a basic block and counter strike combination, absorbing the energy of the attack and redirecting it back at its source. It is merely an application of the universal law of physics which allows one to intercept a line of force and redirect it around the spherical perimeter of the *Chan-Su* (cocoon), projecting it away on a tangential line.

The fourth, and most difficult, principle of the martial arts is that of *Neutralization*. This refers to the countless methods of immobilization, such as joint-locks and pressure point manipulation, which is symbolized by the solidity of the element of *Earth*. The proper application of such techniques requires more focus and control to accomplish than any other aspect of the martial arts. Their difficulty is compounded even more by the possibility of severe injury to the joint if the hold is not properly applied.

Technically, Neutralization is the ability to redirect any incoming line of force along a decreasing spiral, which will turn its power back upon itself. This is quite different from the third principle, that of Projection, in that the defender and/or controller maintains a constant contact with the line of force throughout the movement and redirects it into a static condition.

When we speak of force and the redirection of force, however, we do not mean the application of brute physical strength (*Jing-Li* in Chinese). That would be suicidal. If your opponent were much bigger and stronger than you, it would simply be impossible to overpower him/her. No, instead, the proper application of any tangential form of defense with speed and control will reap the greatest results with the least amount of effort expended.

Speed is power! This is simple physics, and you may see it in operation all about you. It is not the mass of the water that turns the mill wheel. If the water does not move, then neither does the wheel. It is the speed of the flow which makes it useful. A certain amount of mass is necessary, though, or it will not be powerful enough to move the wheel. After all, zero times any number, no matter how large, is still zero. But, it is the velocity and direction of the flow which are the determining factors.

Speed is not a thing which must be developed, however, but a thing to simply let happen. If you try to hard to accomplish anything, your body will tense up from the effort and the contraction (contra-action) of the muscles will hold you back, robbing you of both speed and power. Therefore, keep your physical self in the best possible condition, relax and allow your natural speed to simply appear.

By relaxing completely, not only do you release the devastating power of speed but, also, the unifying force of the *San-Yao*, the Three Powers. The weight of your body settles to rest squarely upon your feet, rooting you firmly to the earth. Your spiritual vitality, or *Shen*, ascends to heaven through the top of your head. It is held as if suspended from the sky by an invisible cord or string. Your intrinsic energy, or *Chi*, sinks into the *Tan-Tien*, the point two or three inches below your navel and one or two inches in front of the spinal column. This is the source of your humanity, your sense of physical and emotional balance.

The ancient concept of the Three Powers, or *San-Yao*, is extremely important to your understanding of the Chinese martial arts. It illustrates the desired condition of humanity living in a state of perfect balance between heaven and earth. From this posture, an awareness of the entire cosmos being engaged in an infinite celestial dance will gradually dawn upon you. The universe has become you, and you are the universe, one and the same, identical and inseparable.

METHODS OF CHINESE YOGA

It was discovered by the ancient Chinese that the spinal cord was the pathway of control and awareness between the mind and the body. Through openings in the vertebral column, nerve fibers connect the brain to virtually every part of the body. But, these openings are being constantly hammered down and narrowed by the relentless force of gravity. Such debilitating effects are further enhanced by poor posture, inactivity, or the bone-jarring impact against the ground produced through improper alignment of the body in motion. And, as these nerve channels are continuously narrowed, the bioelelctrical signals to and from the brain are slowed and weakened, thusly producing poor reflexes and coordination as well as a plethora of subclinical pains.

If one could only conserve the vast amounts of energy that are expended to combat the pull-down of gravity, he/she could possibly extend his/her life by several decades and improve the health of the physical self to near perfection. But, such good spinal posture is not instinctive in humans, as it is in other animals. It must be learned, just as the ability to walk upright must be acquired. This is accomplished by developing the large anti-gravity muscles (legs, abdominals, and back muscles) through a series of focused exercises.

Chinese Yoga, known as *Yu-Chia*, requires none of the heavy equipment or arduous strain associated with weight lifting or isometrics. The muscles are simply tensed in specific patterns and in combination with specific breathing rhythms. The simple movements are executed against an angular self-imposed resistance, making them appear to be almost isometric in nature. But, the muscles are kept in continuous motion, unlike the long holding and blood clotting dangers of isometrics.

Externally, *Yu-Chia* developes the muscles' tissues by forcing them to move against self-imposed resistance. As one becomes stronger, he/she is able to generate greater tension (resistance), which will bring more muscle fibers into action and develop even greater strength.

Internally, deep breathing massages the organs of the body and flushes the entire system with oxygen. This improves the overall health of the musculature, slows the aging process and increases both mental and physical strength.

Correcting misalignments of the spine, caused by poor posture, will not only relieve the vague discomforts which cause much of our confusing behavior, but will also improve the circulation of *Ming* (vital force) throughout the body. This will increase the amount of energy at our physical disposal and add a sense of "quality" to our life.

From just a few minutes to a single hour per day, three to seven days per week, is all that is required to produce a perfect balance of lean tissue and muscle. And, with even a minimum of practice, the vertebral openings will widen and bring renewed life to an aging spine. Blood circulation will improve to every joint of the skeletal system, removing accumulated wastes and lubricating the joints through the gentle stretching of ligaments and tendons. Misalignments of the posture will be corrected, removing the distorted and unflattering picture they have projected to others, allowing them to see the real you as you wish to be, and restoring your lost feelings of self-mastery.

The human body is composed of billions of microscopic cells, each one endowed with enough intelligence and vital energy to accomplish its assigned tasks. Each of these cells belongs to a cell "group," the collective intelligence of which is in direct communication with other similar cell groups, forming a complex network of cellular intelligence under the direct control of the *Instinctive Mind* within the subconscious.

These cell groups function properly and efficiently, unless hindered by the conscious mind through wild displays of emotion or self-destructive habits and practices. They may even be demoralized into retarded or poor operation, or into a full-scale rebellion and strike. Unfortunately, such rebellions can spread throughout the entire cellular network if not immediately stifled and corrected.

Restoration of normal conditions may be accomplished through increased nutrition, exercise and attention. But, correction may be further expedited through direct orders given to the affected cell groups from the focused consciousness. The plan here is to simply "talk" to the rebellious cells, just as you would to a group of unruly children. This may sound ludicrous, but there are many sound scientific reasons behind such a practice. So, do not dismiss it too lightly.

Give the command positively and firmly, repeating the order several times and telling the cells exactly what you expect of them. A gentle tap or a light slap over the affected area will serve to awaken the cell group's attention in much the same way as tapping someone on the shoulder will get their attention.

Please, though, do not suppose that these cells have ears and respond to the spoken word, no matter what language you may use. No, but the sharply spoken command will serve to focus your intentions and transmit them through the network of the central nervous system to the cellular intelligence. What words you choose to speak are not as important as your emotional commitment and sincerity. If you truly mean what you say, your orders will be understood and obeyed to the best of their ability. We think you will be surprised at the amount of control which you actually have over your own body. But, use it wisely!

The cellular life of the body is dependent upon the act of breathing. You may survive for some time without food.

You may even survive for a few days without water. But, without air, your existence can be measured in a matter of heartbeats. To breathe is to live. There can be no life without breathing.

The way you breath is affected by your emotional state of mind. When you are frightened, you will tend to hold your breath. When you are depressed, you tend to inhale more than you will exhale. When excited, you tend to exhale more than you inhale. But, when relaxed and at peace, you breathe more evenly and naturally. Your abdomen expands outward as you inhale and contracts inward as you exhale.

There is an ancient tradition which says that God measures our lives not by years or even days, but by the number of breaths we take. We are permitted only so many inhalation and exhalation cycles with which to live our lives. If we breathe shallow and fast, our lives will be over almost before they have begun, without any purpose or meaning. If, on the other hand, we breathe deep and long, our lives will have greater depth and many more years added to them.

Most people only utilize one or two thirds of their full lung capacity. They either sip little breaths into the top of their lungs with the rise and fall of their shoulders. Or, they throw out their chests and gulp air into the middle third of their lungs. Or, they pump their abdomens in and out to draw the air into the larger bottom third of their lungs. This latter method is the most natural and beneficial of the three, but even it is still limiting.

Proper use of the lungs requires a *Complete Breath*, known in Chinese as *To-Noa* (meaning literally exhale-inhale). This is a combination of all three methods, designed to completely empty the lung cells and then fill them to capacity with fresh air. But, it should be performed in one fluid motion, not in a series of jerky gulps or erratic wheezes.

First, the air cells have to be emptied. The shoulders are drawn slightly down and inward, forcing the air out of the top of the lungs. The muscles of the chest are slowly constricted, squeezing the air out of the middle of the lungs. Then, the diaphragm is thrust upward by sharply drawing in the abdomen, forcing the air up and out. It all works like a giant bellows, only not so exaggerated.

Next, the lungs have to filled again. So, the abdomen is thrust outward, drawing down on the diaphragm and sucking air into the bottom of the lungs. The chest, then, is expanded and the shoulders are thrown back, pulling air into the remainder of the air cells.

Do not hold your breath. Allow the tide of air to ebb and flow naturally, in rhythm with your own heartbeat and your need for oxygen. Once you have this pattern firmly established, you may apply it to the following exercises.

1. CLEANSING BREATH

This is an unbelievably simply exercise that will squeeze stale air and pollutants from the air cells, while also massaging and strengthening the vocal cords. This will improve the basic capacity of your respiratory system and produce a melodic quality to your voice.

Inhale a *Complete Breath* through your nose. But, this time, exhale through your open mouth with an audible "ahh-hh" sound. Tighten not only the chest and abdomen but every muscle of your body as you force the last bit of air from your constricted lungs. Do not inhale until you are no longer able to produce the "ahhhh" sound. Repeat this exercise four more times, using "ehhhh" - "ihhhh" - "ohhhh" - and "uhhhh" sounds.

The Cleansing Breath exercise is quite refreshing when you are feeling all "used up." It will greatly rejuvenate the entire bodily system. It is indispensable for speakers, singers or anyone else who must place great demands upon their voice.

2. RHYTHMIC BREATH

The orbit of the planets, the rise and fall of the oceans, the change of the seasons, even the beat of your own heart,

all motion is but a manifestation of the Divine Law of *Rhythm*.
By tuning your attention to the beat of your own body, you
can open yourself up to the rhythms of the world around you.

This rhythmic time is based upon a unit corresponding
to the beat of your own heart. But, this is the standard for
you and you alone. Each person has his/her own rhythm and
fits into the music of the universe in his/her own way, chang-
ing and modifying the beat from moment to moment.

First, begin the process of a *Complete Breath*, drawing
the air deep into your lungs and counting the beats of your
heart as you do so. You will have to be very still within yourself and listen very carefully for its pulsating voice. Inhale for
a count of four beats, hold the breath for a count of two beats,
and exhale for another four pulses. Hold your lungs empty
for two more beats, then begin the cycle all over again.

With practice, you will be able to increase the duration
of your inhalations and exhalations to six, eight, ten or even
twelve beats of your heart. But, the pauses between breaths
should always be just two beats long.

3. RETAINED BREATH

This exercise is a variation of rhythmic breathing. But,
here you will be increasing the duration of the pauses between the inhalations and exhalations (and vice-versa), while
the length of the breath itself will remain the same.

For example: inhale for a count of four heartbeats, and
hold the breath for a count of four beats, instead of the previous two. Exhale for a count of four heartbeats and hold for
another four pulses. Then, again inhale for four beats, but
hold the breath for a count of six pulses. Exhale for a count
of four and hold your lungs empty for six more beats. Now,
inhale for four beats, again, but hold it for a count of eight.
Exhale for four more beats and hold for another eight. Each
time the pause between the breaths increases by two heartbeats, but the duration of the inhalations and exhalations remains the same.

Unlike the Rhythmic Breathing exercise, where you maintained the same count throughout the entire exercise, the Retained Breath exercise will always increase in duration from a beginning point of four pulses. With practice, you will be able to hold your breath for counts of twenty, thirty, forty, fifty or more heartbeats. Do not, however, continue this exercise to the point that it becomes painful. At the first indication of any true discomfort . . . STOP!!

4. ABDOMINAL BELLOWS

This exercise is a variation upon the Retained Breath exercise which you have just completed. But, now, you will be focusing your efforts into toning and developing the muscles which control the respiration process itself.

For this exercise you will need to stand, with your feet about shoulder width apart and the toes pointed forward. Bend your knees rather deeply and place the palms of your hands upon your thighs just above the knees. Your torso will lean forward at about a forty-five degree angle, but your back must be kept straight. Try to keep the muscles of your body as relaxed as is possible in this position.

Inhale a deep *To-Noa* and hold it. Now, while retaining this breath, pump the muscles of your abdomen in and out as far as possible. Begin slowly and increase the speed of this pumping action, until you are moving the muscles as fast as possible. Do not release the breath as you do this, though.

When you feel as if you simply cannot hold the breath another moment, exhale through your mouth and relax. Stand erect and breathe naturally for a few seconds, then bend forward and repeat the exercise again. Continue until your abdominal muscles are too fatigued to go on, but not until they hurt. At the first sign of any real pain . . . STOP!!

Muscle power is not necessarily proportionate to size. It is not the bulk of a muscle which determines how strong it is, but the number of active fibers which produces the manifestation of strength. An extremely large muscle may have only a few active fibers and, so, be very weak even though it appears very powerful. A rather small muscle, on the other hand, may have a larger number of active fibers and be extremely powerful even though it appears to be weak.

How well the muscle groups work together is another factor which will contribute to its overall strength. One or more muscle must contract to move a limb. One or more muscles must "hold" onto the skeletal structure to support the movement of the limb. And, one or more muscles must function to prevent injury through hyperextension of the joint(s) involved in the action.

Some muscle fibers operate to produce strength, while others will produce speed. These fibers, and the individual muscle groups, must all work together to manifest control, power and speed. No single muscle, or even group of muscles, can ever accomplish this all by itself. The entire body must work together as a single unit if it is to function properly.

It is not always easy to ignore the grumblings of the body, especially when exercising. It is important that you learn to be its master and not let its petty complaints keep you from ever achieving your goals. The physical self can be a lazy creature, if it has never been properly trained and conditioned.

Never cheat on any exercise. Extend or contract the muscle to its fullest. Keep the muscles loose and flexible. This will allow performance of all movements with greater efficiency and speed.

Pain is the language with which the physical self speaks to you and tells when something is not as it should be. That is why it will often produce annoying aches and pains when it is subjected to disciplined exercise. It does not consider such exertion to be a normal condition, and it will tell you so. But, ignore only its petty complaints, not its warnings. If you were to injure yourself, the body would speak to you in this same language of pain but these signals to the brain will be of a very different nature indeed. You must learn to understand this physical language and discern which of its messages to ignore and which to heed. But, in either case, do not shun pain. Remember a simple fact–"Only the dead feel no pain!"

1. SERPENT RIDES WAVES

If you were to perform only one exercise each day for the rest of your life, this should be it! This exercise will improve the flexibility of the spine and combat the effects of gravity, which compresses the sponge-like disks between the vertebrae and pinches the nerves. It will, in turn, improve the posture and allow the internal organs to function more efficiently. It will strengthen the heart and quicken the circulation of blood throughout the entire body. It will, also, improve you sense of balance and grace. (See illustration Figure E-1.)

The feet are placed slightly wider than shoulder width apart, knees slightly bent. The arms swing loosely out to the sides as you inhale a *Complete Breath*. Arch the back, until you can look directly at the ceiling or sky.

Exhaling through your open mouth, curl your body forward and circle your arms inward, until your hands come together and reach backward between your legs. Touch the floor or ground behind you and tense your abdominal muscles, pulling the belly inward.

Then, inhaling through your nose, rise up and arch your back, circling your arms out to the sides. Repeat ten times.

2. CRANE STRETCH

Place your weight on your left leg and fold your right leg up, like a wading bird standing on one leg. Grab you right ankle with your right hand, and inhale a *Complete Breath* through your nose. Using your left arm to control you balance, exhale through your open mouth and push back as hard as you can with your right leg, as if you were attempting to push your ankle out of your own grasp. (See illustration Figure E-2.)

Do not allow the leg to escape from your grip, however, and do not lock your left knee. Keep your supporting leg bent. Relax and, drawing your right foot back towards your buttocks, inhale again through your nose. Repeat the entire cycle three to five times on each leg.

This exercise will stretch the large muscle on the top of the thigh, the quadriceps. But, be careful not to hold this tensed position for more than two or three seconds.

3. TEMPLE DANCER

In this exercise, the palms of the hands are placed together, like an Oriental dancing girl, so that you cannot use your arms to control your balance. Inhale a *Complete Breath* and raise your right leg up in front of you, with the knee slightly bent and the toes pointing upward at the ceiling or sky. Then, squat slowly on you left leg, exhaling slowly through your open mouth. Do not squat too deeply, though. Only lower yourself enough to feel the brunt of your weight transferred onto the quadriceps muscle. (See illustration Figure E-3.)

Hold this position for a few seconds, as you expel the air from you lungs through your open mouth. Then, inhale and straighten your left leg, relaxing the quadriceps. Repeat this exercise three to five times on each leg.

4. SPEARMAN LUNGES

Inhale a *Complete Breath* and take a moderate size step forward with your left foot. Be sure to keep the toes of both feet pointed straight ahead, as if you were walking along a line painted upon the floor or ground. Then, exhaling through your open mouth, shift your weight forward and bend your left knee deeply, like a spearman thrusting his weapon at an enemy. Do not, however, allow your right heel to come up off the floor as your right leg straightens. (See illustration Figure E-4.)

This movement will stretch the long hamstring tendon at the back of the knee, the calf muscle and the achilles tendon at the back of the ankle. But, do not hold this position for more than two seconds before inhaling and shifting your weight back onto the rear leg. Repeat this stretch three times on each leg.

5. PULLING SILK

For this exercise you should assume the *Horse Stance*, known in Chinese as *Ma Bu*. The feet should be placed slightly wider than the span of the shoulders. The toes should point straight forward and the weight should be carried on the outer edge of the feet, causing the legs to round outward as if they were hugging the sides of a horse.

Inhale a *Complete Breath* and extend your arms forward from the shoulders, parallel to the floor and to each other. Your hands should be open and your arms relaxed. Then, exhaling through your open mouth, bend your elbows downward against your ribs and close your hands into tight fists. Rotate the fists so that your knuckles point to the ceiling or sky, and draw down and inward on your shoulders. (See illustration Figure E-5.)

Hold the tension for no more than two or three seconds before inhaling and extending your arms forward. Open your hands and relax. Repeat the entire movement five to ten times. This exercise will strengthen the large pectoral muscles of the chest, and add power to the biceps muscles of the upper arm.

6. CRANE SPREADS WINGS

Cross your arms over your chest as you inhale a *Complete Breath*. Then, as you exhale through your open mouth, swing your arms out and downward at about a forty-five degree angle from your shoulders. Attempt to bend your arms backwards against the natural hinge of the elbows. (See illustration Figure E-6.)

This movement will cause the triceps muscle along the back of the upper arm to cramp into a powerful knot, and the large muscles of the entire upper back to bunch up and contract. But, do not hold this position for more than two or three seconds before inhaling and crossing your arms over your chest again, stretching the muscles after such a powerful contraction. Repeat this exercise five to ten times.

7. DRAGON LIFTS WINGS

The wings of the dragon are quite different from those of the crane. After all, a dragon is not a bird, so its wings are hinged differently. Imitating the dragon will, therefore, exercise an entirely different set of muscles.

Cross your arms over your chest, exactly as you did in the CRANE SPREADS WINGS exercise, and inhale a *Complete Breath*. Then, as you exhale through your mouth, swing your elbows out to the sides and upward towards the ceiling or sky. Your forearms should hang straight down from the elbows, loose and relaxed. But, your shoulders will bunch up and contract as the elbows are pushed higher and higher. Do not, however, thrust the elbows upward in jerky bounces but in a slow and steady ascending motion. (See illustration Figure E-7.)

Hold this position for two or three seconds before inhaling again and crossing your arms over your chest. Repeat this entire movement five to ten times.

8. MONKEY ROLLS

This exercise will massage all of the internal organs and push them back into their proper place. This will reduce the unsightly bulging of the abdomen that is caused by the downward pull of gravity upon these organs. The rolling action is also beneficial to the spine, but this exercise should only be performed upon a padded or carpeted surface to avoid any injury to the delicate vertebrae.

Sit upon the floor or ground, with you knees drawn up and your feet flat upon the surface beneath you. Inhale a *Complete Breath* and pull your knees in sharply with your hands upon your shins, driving them into your abdomen and forcing the air far up into your chest. Suck in your abdomen as far as possible, hold your breath and allow your body to roll over backward. Keep your back rounded and roll well up onto your shoulders. Be careful, however, not to shift your weight too far backward and put undue pressure on your neck. (See illustration Figure E-8.)

Exhale through your open mouth as you reverse directions and roll back into a sitting position. Inhale and repeat the entire exercise five to ten times.

9. LOTUS REACHES TO SUN

This exercise is designed to tone and flatten the muscles of the abdomen, perhaps the most important muscles of the entire body. They are vital to every action physically possible, from lifting and pulling to walking and standing. Without strength in the abdomen, all other forms of strength are useless.

Lie on your back and place your feet flat on the floor or ground, knees bent and feet together. Rest your open palms upon the tops of your thighs and inhale a *Complete Breath*. Then, as you exhale through your mouth, straighten your legs and raise them to a forty-five degree angle above the floor. At the same time, curl your upper body forward and reach for your toes. Do not allow your lower back to come up off the floor, and do not bounce as you stretch towards your feet and tighten your abdominal muscles. (See illustration Figure E-9.)

Hold this position for two or three seconds before inhaling and settling back into a supine position. Bend your knees and place your feet flat on the floor again, sliding your hands back down your thighs. Repeat this action ten to fifteen times.

PROCESS OF MEDITATION

What we see is not what is actually occurring. What we think we see is not necessarily the same image that was registered upon our optic nerves. Our perception of the world around us is colored by the nature of our beliefs. We are constantly interpreting everything that we see, hear, smell, taste, or feel within the framework of these beliefs. Even when we listen to someone describing an experience which is new to us, we consider and judge it according to our current beliefs, assumptions and conclusions.

Our beliefs are not static, however. They are subject to change at any moment. Consider how people of not so long ago thought that the world was flat, and that it was possible to sail right over the edge. This was a major belief that governed how these people dealt with their world. With the discovery that the world was actually round came entirely new concepts of science and space. Even our understanding of time was altered by the discovery that the Earth is a rotating sphere, and that the sun does not circle us but that we orbit it.

Our physical and mental reactions are not to events of the present moment, the *Here and Now*, but to a brief moment of observation in the recent past. This could be a unit of time as small as a fraction of a nanosecond, however, and it would still qualify as a delayed reaction. This delayed reaction becomes even more of a problem when we react as if it were some other event which we had witnessed, an illusion created by the act of misinterpreting the event through the filter of our beliefs.

So, the first requirement for our successful interaction with our environment is getting to the truth of what is occurring around us. We must experience what is actually taking place, on all levels of physical existence, without value judgements or assessments, without alterations or interpretations, without any emotional blinders or filters. We must get beyond the coloring of our beliefs and just experience this moment of Life.

The mineral, plant and animal kingdoms were seen by our common ancestors as inseparable filaments in the complex web of planetary life. Only the human being was capable of stepping out of the grand procession and moving at contrary angles to its unstoppable current. Our sentient consciousness has allowed us the power of creation/destruction over our environment, so it must be this same sentience which will bring us back into rhythm with the Dance of Life.

The human body, and even the gray matter of the brain itself, could be methodically dissected cell-by-cell and not one trace of the consciousness would be found. The brain is simply an instrument for the processing of consciousness. Just as the ears process sound but do not create the tone, or the eyes process light but do not create the radiance, or the lungs process air but do not create oxygen, so does the brain process consciousness but is not its source of origin.

All information received through the five senses, and interpreted by the brain, is processed by the thoughts of the individual's mind, much like an emperor who is forced to receive all knowledge of his empire from his staff of advisors. The emperor will know only what the advisors wish him to know. So, too, do your emotionally charged thoughts and beliefs distort your awareness of the material world received through your five senses. The emperor needs to occasionally escape the control of his advisors and see, hear, touch, smell and taste the wonders of the realm for himself.

But, one cannot experience life from a catatonic sleep. To completely stop the thinking process is to become one of the living dead. This is not, contrary to popular belief, the objective of meditation. It is not a "Blanking Out" of the mind. In fact, it is just the opposite. Meditation is an expansion of the consciousness while, simultaneously, controlling the endless current of thoughts so that life is merely experienced, instead of reacted to and judged by the emotionally motivated psyche.

Meditation is a tool of the mystic. And, mysticism is nothing more than the study of methods and techniques used to directly experience a conscious awareness of the natural laws and cosmic forces governing reality. Actually, anything done with this type of focused awareness is, by definition, a form of meditation. The only requirement is an advanced state of relaxation and tranquility of thought. But, this is often easier said than accomplished.

For many people relaxation of any kind seems to be an unreachable destination. Life is, after all, a stress-filled and painful experience. Is it not? The more it hurts, the more you must resist. But, the more you resist, the more it hurts. Or, is this vicious cycle of self-destruction merely a problem of perception?

Nevertheless, perception or not, if you do not relax from time to time, you will steal years from your already too short life. You must learn the art of *Instant Relaxation*. Remeber that the taut bowstring, which is kept tense and never slackened, will soon become useless. Do not allow your emotions to become stretched as tight as a bowstring. Relax!

"Is such a thing really possible?" many of you may be asking by now. "Instant relaxation. Isn't that a contradiction in terms? Relaxation takes time, like a two week vacation, so how could such a thing be possible?"

Yes, relaxation may be accomplished instantly. But, there is a small matter of semantics here. Relaxation is not a single state of being. It may be subdivided into an infinite number of levels. Thus, it is quite possible to be in a peculiar condition of *Sung* or "relaxed tension." For example: if you had to hold two object together until the glue binding them dried, you would have to maintain just enough tension to assure a snug fit but remain relaxed enough to maintain this tension for a prolonged period of time without tiring.

For a person unaccustomed to just relaxing, any efforts at relaxation will only result in a state of this peculiar relaxed tension. But, with practice, such a person may ease into deeper and deeper levels of relaxation.

Unlike muscular tension, which is limited by the size and density of the muscle fibers and tissues, there are no limits to how much a body may relax. Subtle amounts of tension may be continuously discovered in the muscles and released, creating deeper and deeper levels of relaxation, even for a novice to the process of meditation.

There is an ancient saying in the martial arts that "where the head goes, the body must follow." This is true in a strict psychological sense, too. And, this is the core concept of our first exercise in the experience of relaxation and, eventually, meditation itself.

THE FACIAL FIST

It is much easier to relax muscles from a state of maximum tension than it is to loosen an already slack one. Therefore, we will begin by creating a condition of maximum tension in the muscles of the face.

Crunch your eyes as tightly shut as possible, wrinkling up your nose and furrowing your brow. Clinch your teeth tightly together and feel the muscles of your jaw become rigid. Fold the entire face inward upon itself, like the closing of a large fist.

Hold this contraction for a few seconds. Then, quickly, release the tension from your face and neck. Allow your head to loll forward upon the stem of the spine, and feel your mouth drop loosely open. Slump back against your chair and, for a few moments, just enjoy the peaceful sensation of relaxation flowing down into the rest of your body.

Perhaps the single greatest benefit of this type of exercise is that it may be performed almost anywhere, under almost any circumstances, and requires only a few seconds to efficiently utilize. Even when you have advanced to the highest levels of expertise in the art of meditation, this simple little exercise will still be your most valuable tool.

To understand meditation, you must realize that you are a *Spirit Being* as well as a *physical entity*, and that the mental self or conscious mind is but a combination of these two opposite polarities. This intimate relationship may be thought of as a kind of psychic "sandwich." On the one side you have the lower intellect that controls the autonomic nervous system, glandular response functions and physical stimulus memory. This inner subconscious self is known in Chinese as *Po*. On the other side you have the material manifestation of the infinite Spirit Self,or the superconscious mind, known in Chinese as *Shen*. In the middle is the conscious mind, which fluctuates back and forth between the passive influence of the subconscious mind and the active inspiration of the superconscious mind. This moderating consciousness is known in Chinese as *Hun*.

The psychic energies of these three levels of the conscious self correspond to the three "vital centers" which are known as the *San-Ho* (the Three Rivers). Each one utilizes a separate aspect of the life-force of *Ming*. (See illustration Figure F.)

In meditation, the mysterious energy of *Ming* is circulated through these three centers and forms a living pillar of Light. As the vital force begins to flow outward into the central nervous system, the individual awakens to a sense of peace and well-being. The subconscious will begin to rid itself of undesired feelings and negative thought patterns, calming the conscious mind and clearing it of self-destructive reactionary responses. The unhampered awareness, then, begins to function from the spiritually oriented superconsciousness. Thus, the channel to the *Higher Self* is established.

The ancient masters of the Orient have taught us to transcend all attachment to the gross material self by channeling consciousness through the *Tien-Yen*, the third eye. The physical eyes should actually be turned inward and upward to this mystical point in the middle of the brow.

You are in touch with your world through the physical senses, and the sense of sight is the most compelling sense of all. When you turn your eyes downward, you tend to relate to your world through the subconscious mind. When you look straight ahead, you tend to relate through the conscious mind. And, when you gaze upward, you tend to relate to the physical realm through the Higher Self of the superconscious. Notice that when you are in a very negative mood, depressed or angry, how you turn your eyes downward and your behavior reflects your subconscious thoughts and responses. The next time that you find yourself feeling rather moody, lift your eyes and focus your attention outward through the *Tien-Yen*. Your gloom will fade and you will feel more in control of yourself and the situation.

This fixation upon the third eye is known, in Chinese, as *Ting*. It is the first step toward meditation. It is, then, followed by *Ching*, or the release of attachment to the endless "chattering of the inner monkey," the incessant flow of trivial thought through the river of the conscious mind. This silence leads to a state of peaceful beatitude known as *An*.

But, the silence of *Ching* is not a true state of mental silence at all. The inner monkey cannot be completely quieted, unless it is put to death. Instead, one must learn to hear the silence which transcends its endless chattering. One will never master the gibbering animal through force. However, if one learns to simply ignore the perpetual stream of thoughts which flood the mind, to become detached from their influence, the mind will magically appear to silence itself.

Meditation should promote a feeling of peaceful comfort and security. Your physical posture should, therefore, be secure and comfortable. There are many drawbacks to certain meditational postures, however.

Some people prefer to meditate while laying flat upon their backs. But, the biggest disadvantage to this position is that it is too easy to fall asleep. Others prefer to sit upon the floor and twist their legs unnaturally under their bodies. This position has several disadvantages. First, it will cut off the circulation of blood to the legs and cause painful cramps in the muscles. Secondly, without support for the back, it is too easy to slump forward and put unnecessary strain upon the spine. And, lastly, once the position is successfully locked-in, it is easy to allow the mind to just "drift off."

For any type of seated meditation, we would recommend a comfortable chair with a straight back. Sit well back in the seat, with the spine erect, and keep both feet flat upon the floor. Rest your hands lightly upon the tops of your thighs, palms upward.

But, for this present course of instruction, we recommend the process of *standing meditation.* There are several excellent and important reasons for this. Initially, because standing meditation requires a certain portion of the consciousness to be focused upon maintaining balance, it is very difficult to "drift off" or fall asleep. Secondly, blood circulation is not hindered to any part of the body. In fact, because each posture involves a certain amount of movement, circulation of blood is both improved and strengthened. And, lastly, because standing meditation requires proper body alignment, any discomfort will quickly show where there is any excess tension and a need for further relaxation.

Standing meditation, known as *Chan-Chuang*, is an entirely different process from any other type of focused awareness. It is not an attempt to isolate the mind from the body, as many forms of meditation are. Instead, it unifies the body and mind and Spirit, binding them more closely together and allowing them to function as a more perfectly evolved Being.

After all, they are actually inseparable and should be treated as such, even until death.

The first of the *San-Wen*, or "Three Steadinesses," that the mind/body will go through is a state of "*Trembling*." This will take form, first, merely as an oscillating of the attention, because the untamed mind will rebel against the new restrictions being placed upon it. Next, it will appear as an involuntary quivering of the muscles, because the physical body may not be accustomed to such discipline. But, no matter how frustrating this initial phase may seem at the moment, it will soon pass.

The mind/body will, then, progress through a phase of "*Ice and Fire*." The hands and feet will feel frozen, and the mind will feel numb. Then, suddenly and without warning, the entire body will fell consumed by an inner blaze, and the mind will become an inferno of conflicting logic and emotions. But, do not be frightened, because you are now upon the threshold of a great spiritual awakening. The fire is a sign that the energies of the *San-Ho* have been released into the physical body. They will soon come under the control of the Spirit and settle into a pleasant warmth in the physical self and a calm reflective awareness in the mind. This state is known as *Fan-Chao*.

Fan-Chao is that transcendental state where the mind is unhampered by its own misconceptions and/or anxious expectations. It is, during this phase, ready and able to see the world as it truly is. It will now recognize both the good and the bad, the beautiful and the ugly, but it will not pass judgement upon them or try to alter them in any way. The mind has become a mirror, and . . .

> Because the mirror is colorless, it can reflect the whole world.
>
> — Chinese proverb

If you meditate with your head alone, you will get stuck playing all manner of mind games with yourself. So, instead, you must learn to simply sit, or stand, and just *BE*. Experience the moment, nothing more and nothing less. Experience it with all of your senses–sight, hearing, smell, touch and even taste. But, do not evaluate or judge the input. Allow it to just *BE*.

There are a few rules, however, which should be observed if you wish your *Chan-Chuang* to be successful . . .

1. Your head should feel pulled upward as if by a string and your shoulders should remain down. Your neck should be relaxed in this position, known as *Dung-Tao*.

2. Your elbows should press inward against your ribs, pointing downward. Do not allow them to move too far from this position of *Mai-Jiang*.

3. The back should be kept straight and the pelvis tipped very slightly forward, so that the vertebrae are stacked one atop another. The torso leans neither backward nor does it tip forward, but maintains a complete alignment of the spine in this position of *Ting-Yu*.

4. The weight-bearing foot should remain flat on the floor or ground. Your weight should sink through your knee into the earth, rooting your stance in this position of *Lok-Ma*.

There are four basic types of meditations practiced within the art of *Tai-Yang Lung Tao*, the Way of the Sun Dragon. The first is universal to most all forms of meditation, while the other three may be new to western students who are not yet familiar with the discipline techniques of the ancient Chinese.

BREATH COUNTING

Stand naturally and close your eyes. Focus your gaze outward through the *Tien-Yen*. Listen to the rise and fall of your breathing, but do not consciously direct its flow. Allow it to rise and fall of its own accord. Merely act as an observer.

Now, begin to silently count the number of inhalations, but be careful to carry on no other mental conversation than to simply number each breath. Do not even think about the process of breathing. Or, even the process of counting. Just count!

Number each inhalation up to ten, then begin all over again at one. This sounds much simpler than it actually is. Your mind will attempt to wander away from its task and seek other forms of entertainment. You will find yourself counting to thirteen or fourteen before you realize what has happened. But, do not become disgusted, just start over again at one and count to ten.

In time, Your physical body will go through a remarkable transformation which will create further distractions. But, you must be patient with yourself and not criticize your progress, or lack of progress. After all, anything worth having takes time.

CIRCULATING THE LIGHT

Assume the *Horse Stance*, or *Ma Bu*, which you learned in the last chapter, with the weight evenly distributed between both feet and the legs rounded as if they were hugging the sides of a horse. But, this time, your hands should hang loosely down at your sides. From there they will come together, just below waist level, as you begin to inhale through your nose. They will cross at the wrists, palms upward, and travel upward close to your chest as your lungs fill with air, until they reach shoulder height. Then, as you begin to exhale through your open mouth, they will separate and descend away from your body, palms downward, until they reach waist level, where they will again cross at the wrists and prepare to rise as the tide of your breath changes. (See illustration Figure G-1.)

Once you have this pattern firmly established, close your eyes and focus your attention on the *Tien-Yen*. Looking outward through the brow, see a warm white light ascending through your body, lifted by your inhalation and your open palms. It begins at your groin and ascends upward into the middle of your forehead, through all three energy centers. As you exhale through your open mouth, the light descends outside your body, pushed by your hands, to enter again at the base of the spine and be lifted up through your body once again.

ROTATING THE SPHERE

For this meditation, you will assume the *Bow and Arrow Stance*, known in Chinese as *Kung-Chien Bu.* Take a short step forward with your left foot, turning it sideways so that the toes point to the right, across your body. The toes of your right foot should point toward the instep of your left foot, and your right leg should bear most of your weight. Both feet should be kept flat on the floor. The image here is that of an arrow (your right foot) notched into a longbow (your left foot).

At chest height, your hands should be held about twelve inches apart with the palms curved and facing each other, as if they were holding a large ball. In fact, with the eyes closed and focused through the brow, see this sphere of white light and feel its warmth against your skin. Do not hold it too tightly, however, or it will pop just like a bubble. But, do not hold it too loosely either, or it will slip from your grasp. Image its reality with your mind and feel its resistance with your hands.

Now, as you exhale through your open mouth, push the sphere away from you and slightly upward. Shift your weight onto your left foot as your arms extend forward. Then, as you inhale through your nose, draw the sphere downward and back toward your chest. Shift your weight onto your right foot and bring the sphere up to your chest. (See illustration Figure G-2.)

Continue to rotate the sphere away from you and back as you exhale and inhale rhythmically. Get involved in the reality of your imagery. Give the sphere substance and weight. Continue for as long as you wish, but be certain to practice this meditation in its mirror-image, with the position of your feet reversed.

SPREADING THE LIGHT

For this exercise, you must assume the more complex *Cross Stance*, known in Chinese as *Hsiang-Chiao Bu*. Step directly to the right with your left foot, passing in front of your other foot. Place it flat on the floor with the toes pointing forward. Shift your weight onto the left foot, and allow the heel of your right foot to come up off the floor so that only the ball of the foot and toes touch the ground. The right knee should lightly rest upon the top of the left calf muscle. Keep your knees well bent and imagine that your legs are the roots of a great tree, twisted into the heart of the Earth.

Hold your hands in front of your chest with the palms pressed together prayer-style as you inhale a *Complete Breath*. Then, as you exhale through your open mouth, push your hands upward and out to the sides, palms turned outward. Focus your eyes upon the *Tien-Yen* and visualize the white light streaming out from the centers of your palms as they transcribe enormous arcs away from you. Continue to circle your hands and, as you again inhale through your nose, allow them to descend until they come together at waist level. Press the palms together, hold your breath for a brief instant, and draw your hands back up to your chest. (See illustration Figure G-3.)

Continue to circle your arms up, out and down to the sides as you inhale and exhale in rhythm to the movement. See the entire world around you being bathed in your light and love. Feel your heart unfold each time your arms are spread wide, as if you wished to embrace the universe and draw all life into your heart each time your arms close again. Prolong the experience as long as you wish, but be certain to practice its mirror-image, with the position of your feet reversed.

DANCE OF THE SUN DRAGON

The martial art of *Tai-Yang Lung Tao* is one of the purest simplicity, but it is complex in its simplicity . . . and simple in its complexity.

The entire art of the Sun Dragon is embodied in a single, extremely simple movement, which takes the form of a fluid serpentine dance. And, although this one precisely preset dance will appear to be exactly the same for each person who practices this art, the endless journey into Infinity is still a uniquely individual experience and the number of techniques or variations which may be extracted from its single movement are limited only by the depth of the individual's own self-awareness.

The performance of the physical form is a conscious focus upon the balance between the internal and external forces of one's own personality. This becomes an outer manifestation of the *Pa-Kua*, the eight trigrams of the *I-Ching*. It teaches the practitioner to generate four types of *Fa-Jing*, or kinetic energies, which begin as an emotional response expressed through the physical body. In this type of internal training, emotional content takes precedence over physical technique. The ultimate goal of this type of training is, therefore, to learn to move with such power and balance that you can unconsciously merge with and control any external force, while still preserving your own.

The internal martial arts of China require that the Spirit and not the mind direct the movements of the body. It is only when the physical self obeys, effortlessly, that the life-force energies of *Jing* and *Chi* will flow freely. Your strength should, therefore, always emanate naturally from your Inner-Being. This kind of awareness is not a piece of clothing which you may put on and take off at will. It is more like your skin, which is a part of you until death, and causes your whole being to move as one.

But, before you may begin to develop this type of awareness, through the Dance of the Sun Dragon, you must first center yourself and show proper respect to *Tai-Yang Lung*. This is done in the form of a meditative "SALUTATION TO THE RISING SUN."

The feet should be planted slightly wider than the span of the shoulders. Take three or four long, deep breaths and close your eyes, turning your sight inward. Then, opening your eyes, bring your hands together in front of you at waist level and form a triangle with the tips of your thumbs and index fingers. This triangle is symbolic of the Divine Trinity of positive, negative and neutral which keeps the entire universe in eternal balance.

In unison, your hands rise up at arms length and your eyes focus upon the space in the center of the triangle. This action represents your spiritual vision being directed outward from your center, balanced and harmonized, as you rise through the many realms of the Universe of Universes. When your hands reach a point approximately forty-five degrees above your line of vision, allow them to stop.

Next, your hands separate and your arms circle out to the sides. Continue this slow descent, in a giant arc, until your hands meet again at waist level. Now, press their palms together as if in prayer and bring them up in front of your lightly bowed face. This motion symbolizes the expansion of your awakened consciousness and, through its enlightenment, the gathering of all creatures into your heart. (See illustration Figure H-1.)

Once this salutation is completed, stand quietly for a few moments and contemplate its divine significance. Do not, however, focus upon your many mistakes of the past or your numerous hopes for the future. Feel only this moment.

You may now begin the single movement known as DRAGON CIRCLES THE SUN. (See illustration Figure H-2.) But, until you become comfortable with this movement, do not attempt to move your feet. Simply shift your weight from side to side from the *Horse Stance*, or *Ma Bu*, as you circle your arms.

As you shift to the left, your left forearm is held horizontally near your face and the elbow will lead your torso as it pivots upon your waist to the left. The right forearm is held vertically, forming an open ninety degree angle at your hands.

Then, as you pivot back to the right, your left elbow will drop down and your right elbow will rise up, so that your right forearm is now held in a horizontal position near your face and your left forearm is now held in a vertical position. Your hands will still form the same open ninety degree angle, which serves as the circular hub around which your forearms rotate.

Practice this undulating movement from left to right, and from right to left, until you are able to continue it without any conscious thought or direction. If one leg becomes heavy as you shift your weight from side to side, the other leg must become light. If one arms goes up, the other must go down. If your hands are held wide open, they are *"Double Yang."* But, if they are completely closed, they are *"Double Yin."* To achieve perfect balance, the hands must be kept half-open/half-closed. If the muscles of the body are too tense, you will be *"Double Yang"* and unable to flow properly. But, if they are too loose, you will be *"Double Yin"* and collapse. To find balance, the body must be both hard and soft at the same time, like "steel covered with cotton." Then, and only then, will you be ready to begin.

This *Wu-Hui*, or dance, is based upon the complex numerology of the ancient *I-Ching*. Its *Kuen*, or pattern, forms the eight point *Star of the Pa-Kua.* (See illustration Figure H-3.) There are four separate pivots performed with the feet, which represent the Four Elements of Air, Fire, Water, and Earth that are the building blocks of the universe. And, the entire dance is performed twice, symbolic of the twin polarities of *Yin-Yang.* If you total together the number of times each point of the star is touched upon, therefore, the sum will equal the sixty-four hexagrams of the *I-Ching.*

$$8 \times 4 \times 2 = 64$$

Visual aids are indispensable training tools in any form of martial arts. These aids may be either tangible or intangible in nature. Tangible visual aids could be the illustrations of a book or the actual physical demonstration of an instructor. But, intangible aids can only be found in the realm of the mind itself. They take the form of strongly visualized images which relate directly to the physical practice of the art, such as the visualization of the life-force during the performance of *Yu-Chia* or *Chan-Chuang.*

Before performing the Dance of the Sun Dragon, the student should first picture him/herself standing in the middle of a large eight point star that has been etched into the floor or ground beneath his/her feet. As he/she moves around the star from the starting point, having a knowledge of exactly where the other points of the star are in relation to his/her present position will help him/her to perform the movements with a more definite sense of direction and meaning.

Begin with your right foot upon the dot at the center of the star. Your left foot should be placed upon the western point of the star. In china, you would begin with your left foot upon the easter point, so that you would face to the south, but it is much easier for westerners to maintain their bearings if they begin facing north. However, if you wish to utilize the more traditional orientation to the south, please do so. The direction of your starting point is not as important as achieving perfect form. For this manual, though, we shall refer to all directional changes from a northern point of alignment.

Perform the SALUTATION TO THE RISING SUN and, then, begin the movement of DRAGON CIRCLES THE SUN by pivoting your upper body to the right. Pivot to the left, reversing the position of your arms and shifting your weight to the left. As you pivot back again to the right, drop your right elbow and, at the same time, lift your left foot up beside your right knee and step back behind you to the southeastern point of the star. Pivot again to the left and allow the movement of your arms to rotate you upon the balls of your feet until you face the southwest, one hundred thirty-five degrees from your point of origin.

Do not hesitate or pause, but continue this 1-2-3-4 rhythm by pivoting your upper body to the right then to the left and back to the right again. On the count of three, exchange the positions of your arms and lift your left foot up beside your right knee again. Step back to the northern point of the star and pivot upon the count of four until you are facing east, another one hundred thirty-five degrees from your last position.

Since all movement and power is directly dependent upon one's connection to the Earth, the relationship between your stance and the floor or ground beneath your feet is of primary importance. Practice walking through the *Pa-Kua Star* while maintaining a profound mental imagery. See yourself standing perched upon two vertical poles. Your orientation and manner of thinking will have to change from that of a body moving along horizontally across the surface to one of a spherical structure rolling its way along by endlessly shifting its center of gravity vertically from one point of contact to another. A sphere's center and its single point of contact with the ground always forms a perpendicular line to the surface beneath its mass. This line is an ever-present constant as its center of gravity glides along an unwavering distance from the surface. Your weight is pressed straight down into the top of each imaginary pole. And, if the image is visualized strongly enough in the mind that each pole is extremely tall, not only will you achieve a greater depth of feeling in your stances but also an increased incentive to stay on the pole and not lose your balance.

Although your motions may seem awkward and jerky during these first attempts at the dance, be patient and they will smooth out and become graceful. For the moment, though, continue rotating your arms and stepping back one hundred thirty-five degrees around the pattern. This will carry you through the eight directions of the *Pa-Kua Star* in a very specific sequence.

You will, then, conclude this phase of the *Wu-Hui* (dance) with the SALUTATION TO THE SETTING SUN. This is nothing more than a reversal of the SALUTATION TO THE RISING SUN. It begins with the hands held prayer-style in front of the face once again, where they will descend together to waist level and break apart to circle out to the sides. They will continue to circle upward until they meet at a position about forty-five degrees above your line of vision, where they will again form a triangle and descend to below waist level. Your eyes will follow the progress of this triangle and, as your hands finally part, you will finish with your head bowed.

Do not attempt the other three versions of this dance until you can perform this one with a bare minimum of conscious thought and direction. Refer often to the illustration of the *Pa-Kua Star* and trace the path of your steps upon its lines with your eyes. You may even wish to put some tape marks upon the floor, measured by the width of your own stance.

Once you are comfortable with this first phase of *Tai-Yang Lung Wu-Hui* (the Dance of the Sun Dragon), you may perform it in its mirror-image. Instead of stepping back with your left foot and pivoting to your right, you will now step back with your right foot and pivot to your left. Remember, however, that this will reverse the order in which you face the Eight Directions.

Next, when you feel proficient at these two patterns, you will again begin the movement of DRAGON CIRCLES THE SUN. But, this time, you will step forward and across in front of the foot placed in the center of the star, not behind it. For example: if you step forward with your left foot from its starting place upon the western point of the star, you will step across to the northeastern point and pivot to face the southeast. However, in order to utilize the momentum and direction of your arms to make this turn, you will have to reverse the coordination between the raising of your foot and the drop of your elbow. Where your right elbow had to drop down against your ribs as your left foot stepped back behind you and your arms slid you around to the left, now your left elbow will drop down as your left foot steps across in front of you and your arms will lead you around to the right. This sounds a lot more complicated than it actually is. Be patient, practice slowly and you will soon master it.

Study the pattern of the *Pa-Kua Star* carefully and you will see how the left forward step moves you clockwise, or *Shun-Chan*, around the eight directions (north, southeast, west, northeast, south, northwest, east, southwest and back to north). Then, place your left foot at the center of the star and observe how a right forward step pivots you counterclockwise, or *Ni-Chan*, around the star (north, southwest, east, northwest, south, northeast, west, southeast and back to north).

Eventually, you will be able to perform all four pivots as a single flowing movement, with very little conscious thought or direction. Remember, though, to perform the SALUTATION TO THE RISING SUN at the beginning of the first pattern only. Each of the other patterns should flow into the next without any pause or hesitation. Do not think of each pattern as separate from the rest. See them as colors which gradually shade into each other, until you are no longer certain where one movement ends and the next one begins. It is only after the repetition of all four patterns that you may perform SALUTATION TO THE SETTING SUN.

When you have spent sufficient time mastering the four patterns of DRAGON CIRCLES THE SUN, which forms the *Yang* half of the DANCE OF THE SUN DRAGON, it is time to learn the four *Yin* patterns. They are, essentially, the same as the four pivotal rotations of the *Yang* patterns. The major difference lies in the circling action of the arms, reversed from their position above the horizon of your center (the solar plexus) to a position below this central horizon. This new pattern of movement is known as *Dragon Circles the Moon.* (See illustration Figure H-4.)

Although the *Yin* form may appear quite different, it is actually so similar to the *Yang* patterns that you should have very little trouble mastering its reversed flow. The pattern of your steps will remain exactly the same, and even the shifting rhythm of your weight from side to side remains consistent. The only new aspect to be learned is the raising of your elbows, instead of dropping them against your ribs as you change directions.

Again, this is something which sounds much more complicated than it actually is. We will not, therefore, confuse you with a lot of descriptive explanations. Instead experiment with it, slowly and patiently, and you will soon understand that this is not a separate movement at all, but a reflective parallel, much like your own reflection in the calm waters of a small pool.

When you practice, however, do not allow your mind to wander away to other matters. Do not daydream or imagine yourself in combat with an invisible enemy, which seems to be a very common mistake of many martial arts. Instead, concentrate your attention upon your own body and the feeling each movement creates within it. Do not be concerned with applications or various techniques and combinations. Just flow with the movement and allow it to become your natural, instinctive way of motion. Let the dance become a form of moving meditation.

A peculiar awareness will eventually unfold upon you, in time, that the entire universe is engaged in an infinite cosmic dance and that you are its *Hsu-Jing*, the stillness at the heart of its movement. The universe and you are one, interconnected and virtually inseparable. You are the movement and the movement is you.

Awareness and knowledge gained in this manner is like "snow flakes falling into a pot of water." They will magically become an invisible part of you, hidden somewhere beneath the reflective surface of your thoughts. When their unique individuality comes forth, usually during a time of crisis, their appearance will startle you as much as your opponent. It is much easier, after all, to forget what we have than it is to overlook what we do not yet possess. Desire is often more compelling than memory.

PRACTICAL ANATOMY

A knowledgeable explorer will never dash off into the unexplored wilderness without first making adequate preparations or, at the very least, spending sufficient time examining every detailed map of the region. So, to, should you never even contemplate taking any action against another human being before you completely understand the moral and/or legal consequences of your decision. Ignorance of basic anatomy could transform an act of self-defense into a lengthy jail sentence for excessive use of violence or even manslaughter. Neither a court of law nor your own conscience recognizes the negligent lack of information as an excuse for severely injuring another individual, who may or may not have intended you bodily harm. Granted, a certain amount of force is required to protect yourself from assault, but it is difficult to prove that you only meant to subdue your assailant with a harmless joint-lock when his/her elbow is shattered.

If attacked, there could be an occasion when you are forced to harm your opponent to the point of dislocating or breaking a joint or bone. Should such desperate measures be necessary to save yourself, do not hesitate to do so. But, be aware that persons under the influence of alcohol and/or drugs are very likely to be insensitive to pain and injury. Even a broken arm may not deter his/her assault upon you. Therefore, knowledge of anatomy becomes vital to selecting alternate courses of action.

Defensive techniques and targets of application should be chosen with great care. You must always strive to do the least amount of harm necessary to end an altercation, both legally and ethically. However, when confronted with the reality of street violence, it is *"better to be judged by twelve than carried by six."* So, choose your targets and techniques of physical manipulation with a tendency toward extreme caution, without being reckless or brutal.

Developing high standards of spiritual morality and ethics is an important aspect of training in *Tai-Yang Lung Tao.* Thus, the student should seek to acquire as much understanding of human anatomy as he/she can, in relation to his/her personal defense. This knowledge, then, should be applied to the selection of the defensive applications and body targets in accordance with a strict philosophy of priority. (See illustration Figure I.)

The multiple points along the arms and legs of the figure are listed as number ONEs because, firstly, they are the easiest targets to reach and, secondly, because any damage sustained is usually easy to mend without surgery or extensive therapy. Wrist and elbow locks are the most commonly employed techniques, since most attackers will reach out to grab you with their hands first or thrust a balled-up fist at you. With his/her arm as the closest target, it only makes good sense to take full advantage of such a "gift."

Whenever applying any type of joint-lock, though, be careful to use just enough force to neutralize his/her actions. Joint-locks can be very damaging and you do not want to go beyond what is reasonably necessary to subdue your opponent. The law, too, requires that a person use only enough force to successfully defend him/herself. The use of excessive violence, even in pure self-defense, is illegal!

If you are forced to separate or dislocate any joint, however, it should never be reset on the scene. Nerves and/or blood vessels could be pinched or even severed. This type of first aid should only be performed by qualified medical personnel.

The eight major target points of the body (two each of wrists, elbows, shoulders and knees) are known in Chinese as the *Pa-Men*, or the Eight Gates. Their hinges were designed to swing primarily in one direction only. If you apply enough force against their direction of swing, you will cause extreme pain or even a separation of the joint itself. So, be very careful to apply only enough force to subdue, not cripple.

The wrist is a modified ball-and-socket type joint, similar to the shoulder joint. It is an important target in any kind of grappling, especially torquing or hyperextension techniques. But, although wrist locks are quite effective, they normally require years of practice to apply correctly. They must be learned to near perfection because they are so easily broken and countered, especially if your opponent is rather strong.

The elbow is a hinge type joint. It is more susceptible to locking and twisting techniques than the wrist. However, nerve and blood vessel injuries occur quite often in trauma injuries to the elbow joint.

The shoulder is also a ball-and-socket joint. It is capable of an amazingly wide range of motion, but it is also extremely susceptible to painful separations. In fact, joint dislocations occur more frequently here than in any other joint of the body.

Should the situation be more serious, such as our previous example of the assailant under the influence of alcohol or drugs, the illustrated points upon the legs would become your primary targets. Injuring the knee from the front or side requires a lot less pressure than you might suppose. And, once the knee joint is no longer functional, whether your attacker is able to feel the pain or not, he/she will not be able to stand or follow you as you make your escape. In most cases, however, your attacker will still have some residual awareness of pain. A sharp strike to the unprotected shin bone or a simple stomp to the instep of the foot will be extremely painful and could easily cripple an assailant.

Several points upon the torso are listed as number TWOs because they could cause more serious damage and are, therefore, much less desirable as defensive targets. Unfortunately, there are some situations which call for drastic reactions. Life does not often conform to our philosophies or our expectations. In such instances, a downward strike to the collarbone may easily fracture or break it completely. An upward strike to the solar plexus can temporarily paralyze the diaphragm and restrict breathing. The lower set of floating ribs may be easily damaged by an inward strike with the heel of the hand. Or, a sharp impact to the breastbone will be extremely painful due to the obvious lack of any cushioning muscle.

Any point upon the head, listed here as number THREEs would be struck only when all else has failed and only in the most dire, life-threatening situation. This is not merely because a blow to the head could prove fatal, since it is not always as easy to kill as one might imagine. Although the possibility of death does exist, the main reason for avoiding strikes to the head is more a matter of respect than of safety.

No matter what a person has done, no matter how evil he/she may seem, we must still respect the SPIRIT SELF. In the realm of the Spirit, we are all truly One, perfect and incapable of any error. It is only the finite and limited personality of the physical self which commits the crime against you, not the Spirit Self. And, since the bioelectrical impulses of the brain are the tools with which the Spirit is bound to the physical body, any strike to the head would be an attack upon the Spirit Self. Therefore, out of deepest respect, one should limit all defensive measures to those which do the least amount of damage and will not destroy the connection between the Spirit and the body.

Pulling the hair can be an extremely painful and effective means of control. As we saw earlier, "where the head goes the body follows." Plus, it is the least damaging counterattack that you may aim at the head. Or, if there is not enough hair to grab, the heel of the hand pushed upward under the point of the chin may snap the head back painfully.

A sharp strike to the hinge of the jaw, just below the ear, or slapping the ears with the cupped hands will stun your opponent and may end the confrontation. Almost any kind of strike to the nose will break the delicate cartilage, causing the eyes to water and blinding the attacker. Extreme caution should be exercised when striking the nose, however, since a broken or even a bleeding nose may hinder the assailant's breathing and cause him/her to suffocate.

No matter how muscular you opponent may be, his/her body has many other naturally weak and vulnerable areas. Study carefully the many "hollow" and unprotected spots upon your own physical body, visualizing how best to defend such spots and how to efficiently manipulate them on your adversary.

DEFENSIVE APPLICATIONS

Before you can apply any form of self-defense, you must have a working knowledge of the bodily weapons at your disposal and their possible limitations. And, the most powerful weapon of all is the human mind itself. It is capable of receiving and processing thousands of bits of information every second, both internalizing and storing it away for future reference. This is, in essence, the process of learning. As you master a skill or task, the total brain capacity necessary to perform the action(s) "switches" from large regions where conscious attention and/or supervision are required to much smaller areas of automatic reflex response. The conscious mind is, then, free to engage itself in new challenges.

Unfortunately, this "switch" is normally kept in the off position or not allowed to function properly. Most forms of martial arts training teach you, over a period of many years, to keep it turned off. If your unconscious reflexes have been trained, through endless repetition, to always control the impact of your techniques, you will most likely do the same thing and "pull your punch" when a real fight occurs. Too much conscious thought and concentrated control, like that imposed during limited contact practice with a partner, will program your inner reflex response to keep the switch turned off.

Flipping your subconscious switch to the one position is a lot easier than you may think. The key is visualization, or focused imagination. You can stimulate your instinctive mind with purely imagined input that you would not want to acquire through actual experience. You would not, for example, wish to confront a vicious and armed assailant in the real world. But, through the practice of imaginative visualization, you may safely program your subconscious mind to respond to such an attack in any number of ways.

The subconscious self cannot distinguish between reality and fantasy. That is why it will cause you to physically react to a vivid dream, especially a bad nightmare, as if it were really happening. It does not judge the validity of the information it receives, merely stores the data and/or generates appropriate reactions to the situational stimulus.

Program your mind, just as you would a computerized security system, to follow a few simple rules. It alone is responsible for success in the highest of all forms of defense, the perception and prevention of violence.

AT HOME:

1. Locks, deadbolts and security chains should be installed and used at all times, not just when you are away from home.

2. Keep all curtains and drapes closed at night to prevent curious eyes from observing your actions.

3. Secure identification from any person unknown to you before opening your door to them.

4. Install windows or a security viewer (a.k.a. "peephole") in any exterior door.

5. Keep bushes and trees trimmed away from all windows and entrances.

ON TELEPHONE:

1. Do not give out your name or address to anyone, no matter who they say they are.

2. Do not tell anyone that you are home alone.

IN AUTOMOBILE:

1. Keep doors locked at all times and the windows securely rolled up, especially at night, and never pick up hitchhikers.

2. Keep your car in good running condition and avoid a breakdown in some out-of-the-way place.

3. Park your car only in well illuminated areas.

WHILE WALKING:

1. Stay in the center of the sidewalk, away from the curb or any doorways where an assailant may lurk.

2. Travel only in well illuminated areas, and never travel alone, especially at night.

3. Avoid contact with strangers, and do not be fooled by appearances. Most often, murderers and rapists are well dressed and sophisticated people.

4. Always let someone know where you are going and when you plan to be back.

If, even after observing all of these precautions, you are still a victim of violent assault, your first reaction should be to RUN AWAY!! Or, if escape is not possible at the moment, avoid being hit at all costs. Pivot away from the line of attack and seek an avenue of escape immediately. You may even have to squat under a strike aimed at your head or leap over a blow aimed at your legs.

However, an assault will often happen so suddenly that escape is just not possible. Under such circumstances, you will be forced to respond with some manner of physical reaction corresponding to one of the four elemental manifestations. Each response is a direct reflection of the psychological effect of that particular element to outside stimulus. Each response is a type of *Fa-Jing*, or kinetic energy rising up from the *Tan-Tien* (your center) and colored by the emotions of the moment.

Whether it is a violent assault, a friendly competition of some sort, a business transaction or a conversational debate, the general attitude and physical response will remain consistent in its nature. There are, though, appropriate and inappropriate reactions to any given situation, based upon the philosophic and moral character of the immediate environment.

Each elemental response originates from the "natural posture" known in Chinese as *Hun-Yuan Kung*, which is symbolic of the neutral void of *Wu-Chi* from which all things in the material world were born. It is a relaxed standing posture. The feet are placed slightly less than shoulder width apart with the weight evenly distributed between both. The knees are kept slightly flexed, so that the body's stability is controlled by the powerful muscles of the thighs. The arms hang loosely at your sides and your eyes gaze straight ahead with a soft, distant focus, which will allow you to see everything around you without concentrating upon any one specific point.

1. EARTH (physical awareness): You hold your ground without any superfluous movement. The hips become the center of consciousness and motion, settling you into the earth like a stone.

2. WATER (emotional awareness): You shift and flow like the ocean, receding from the assault in an evasively circular movement and crashing back like a tidal wave to inundate your opponent. The lower abdomen becomes your center of consciousness and motion.

3. FIRE (dynamic energy): Your whole body has a slightly tensed and explosive feel to it as you consume your assailant like a brushfire. The more he/she beats at you,

the hotter you flare up. The solar plexus is now the center of motion and consciousness, the base from which you launch an inferno of strikes and kicks.

4. AIR (intellectual awareness):   Your movements are extremely light and open, receiving and neutralizing the attack without causing any undue harm. The heart is the center of consciousness and motion, allowing you to "float" above all forms of aggression.

Instead of concentrating upon what you are going to do, which specific technique you will apply to this particular situation, simply observe your assailant's actions from *Hun-Yuan Kung* (natural posture) and respond according to your own inner elemental feelings. Be completely involved in the activity of the moment, both physically and mentally. Do not allow your awareness to slide backward into the past of memories or forward into the future of anticipation.

Tai-Yang Lung Tao is an art of neutralizing aggression, blending with energies, disrupting the balance and power of an assault. Your role in such defense appears to be more like manipulating and directing the flow of your opponent's force than merely deciding which technique to apply against his/her attack.

Proper defensive applications borrow the assailant's own energy and uses it against him/her by blending into the line of attack and, then, redirecting its force back to its point of origin or away upon a widening tangent. For example: when someone thrusts a fist at you, merely step to one side and redirect the force of the blow past you along a circular line into the vacant space where there is no resistance to its forward momentum. This is known as *Tsou* or, literally, "to lead by walking away."

Circular motion, called *Yuan* in Chinese, generates considerably more power than linear motion. This can be easily proven by simply observing the forces of nature. A steady, straight flow of water may be navigated without too much difficulty, no matter how deep or swift. But, the circular movement of a whirlpool or the swirling current of an undertow will wreak havoc with any craft or the strongest swimmer. A straight and steady wind will rarely do much damage, but a tornado or hurricane will cause total and utter destruction in an almost effortless manner.

Human beings, however, do not normally generate such effortless power without considerable training. They must progress through a series of stages toward that which should come naturally. The first level is the development of *Jing*, the explosive power of the physical body. Then, the inner strength of continuous energy flow, or *Chi*, is achieved. Lastly, the student accomplishes ultimate spiritual control, or *Shen*, and discovers the essence of effortlessness, known in Chinese as *Wu-Wei*.

When a student executes his/her first truly effortless technique, he/she will rarely believe it. The opponent must have simply allowed the technique to succeed without resistance. It all seems far too easy, too unreal. In fact, it feels as if the attacker actually helped it to happen.

Although we must, out of necessity, establish specific techniques and categories of techniques for the application of this effortless power, there is really only one possible way to physically generate effortless power. It is by allowing your body weight to compress vertically into the earth, but only enough to contract the large muscles of the legs and prepare them to recoil, much like the compression and release of a large spring, and using the resulting power to redirect the incoming force of your opponent's attack into either an outward spiral around the perimeter of your *Chan-Su* (silk cocoon), away from you and back to its source in the form of a counterattack, or into an inward spiral around its own line of movement and downward into a static condition.

There are, however, any number of ways to categorize the infinite methods of applying this one technique. But, for the sake of simplicity, *Fong Su-Yi* translated all possible techniques and their infinite variations into eight basic classifications, or "Characteristics of Defense," symbolized by the eight trigrams of the *I-Ching.*

1. PENG (ward off)   trigram: KUN (earth)

The characteristic of *Peng* may best be visualized as a toy balloon inflated with air. When you push in upon it, the elastic quality of the sphere reacts, redirecting the force of the blow and not letting its energy get through to its center. To employ this same principle, you must respond in a like fashion.

The rotating movement of the waist found in the *Wu-Hui* of the Sun Dragon may be utilized to create a feeling of expansion and to generate a powerful *Yang* (centrifugal) force that will reroute any incoming force around the perimeter of your *Chan-Su* in much the same way that a ping-pong ball thrown at a spinning top is rebounded. The open palm may, then, be used in a simple slapping technique, or *Pak*, to redirect the course of the strike in conjunction with the twisting of the torso. (See illustration Figure J-1.) Or, if you wish to direct the force along an outside line in the opposite direction, you may use the back of the wrist in a simple hooking technique known as *Ou.* (See illustration Figure J-2.) In either case, though, you should always endeavor to "turn the corner" and place yourself on your opponent's blind side, beyond the reach of his/her arms and in control of his/her balance.

The Earth trigram represents your expansive but steadfast attitude. You hold your ground and easily deflect any force which attempts to uproot you.

2. LU (roll back)   trigram: KEN (mountain)

Whereas the energy of *Peng* is solidly planted to the earth and expansive (*Yang*), the energy of *Lu* is more flowing and contractive (*Yin*). It is like the movement of the Earth's surface that presses inward upon itself and, consequently, pushes upward to form majestic mountain ranges. *Lu* is born from the potential of *Peng.*

Once your opponent is committed to his/her course of attack, he/she may be easily led by sinking and turning your body with your legs and waist in the direction of his/her line of incoming force. Your opponent, then, will feel drawn forward into the spiral vacuum by this motion of *Tsou,* or "leading by walking away." (See illustration Figure K.)

Roll Back begins as a Ward Off, performed with the palm either outward or inward–depending upon whether you use the palm or the back of the wrist to deflect the strike –then it turns inward to develop the energy of *Lu,* encircling the attacking limb and maintaining control of it. Unlike *Peng,* where you redirected the assailant away from you, *Lu* requires you to stay in contact with your opponent through the subtle practice of *Nien,* sticking and adhering.

3. CHI (press down)   trigram: KHAN (water)

Often an attack will be initiated with a grabbing technique of some type, or *Lo* in Chinese. As a matter of fact, a recent study has shown that seventy to eighty percent of all assaults began as grabs. When this happens, it is vital that you either release yourself from the trap and escape or, at the very least, reverse the situation and apply some form of neutralization. You must become like water, flowing and swirling out of any hold.

A grab to your arms or wrists, whether from the front or sides, may be released by simply "flicking" it away. This is accomplished by twining your hand and wrist, like the head and neck of the dragon, around the wrist and/or forearm of your opponent's attacking arm. But, in order to effortlessly escape, you must coil about his/her arm in the direction of its least resistance, the single digit of the thumb. (See illustration Figure L-1.)

The dragon will easily coil itself out of any trap. Yet, it does not require brute strength or even speed to succeed. Its movements are relaxed and fluid.

You may reverse the hold upon your opponent by simply helping him/her to maintain his/her grip upon your arm with a hand pressed down on top of his/her and, then, applying a torquing pressure to the wrist or elbow by twining around the arm in the direction of maximum resistance, the strong cluster of fingers. (See illustration Figure L-2.) You do not want him/her to let go of your arm. But, if you opponent should attempt to escape, it will make little difference. Just grab his/her open hand with your own, which you had placed over it for just such an occasion, and maintain a steady pressure upon his/her bent wrist as well as upon his/her locked-out elbow.

The entire process of *Chi* (press down) is a continuation of the inward, centripetal spiral of energy begun by *Lu* (roll back). This vortex swirls inward until it reaches a static, neutral state.

4. TSAI (pull down)   trigram: SUN (wind)

The characteristic of *Tsai* may be visualized as a great downdraft of wind, so strong that it will ground even the mighty eagle. It is used to bring the force of an incoming attack either downward in a decreasing spiral or outward in an increasing arc. The first is utilized to take your opponent to the floor and neutralize him/her, while the second is useful to project him/her bodily away from you and, hopefully, open up an avenue of escape.

Tsai will not be successful, however, if you depend solely upon the strength of your arms to take down your assailant, especially if he/she is larger and stronger than you. The body must function as a total unit, relying upon the waist and legs to control the spiral drop of your weight. A balance stance is vital, sitting down upon the legs and keeping your elbows tucked in against your ribs as you guide the line of your opponent's force with your hands into an inward spiral (see illustration Figure M-1.) or outward into a throwing technique, known as Kwou in Chinese. (See illustration M-2.)

The practice of *Nien* (adhering) and *Tsou* ("leading by walking away") will cause your attacker to feel drawn around you like a leaf in a whirlwind. But, remember to always follow the path of your opponent's trajectory with your eyes. If you do not, your concentration will falter and wander away to other matters of less importance, and you will find yourself becoming uprooted, caught in the current of an unexpected reaction.

And, of course, you should always be prepared to seize the moment and follow a takedown technique with either a Press Down form of neutralization or escape.

5. LIEH (split)   trigram: TIEN (heaven)

The quality of *Lieh* may best be thought of as the angles necessary to fall a tree. Cuts must be made both high and low on opposite sides of the tree, toppling it in the direction of the bottom cut. When executed correctly, *Lieh* will make your assailant fall either backward or sideways to the ground with his/her feet going in one direction and his/her head in another.

First, you will apply *Peng* (ward off) with the back of your left wrist against a right-hand attack or the back of your right wrist against a left-hand attack. Your hand will, then, roll over and grasp your assailant's arm, twisting it at the wrist and hyperextending his/her elbow. Next, stepping behind him/her, you use your other arm to strike or push against his/her chest. This move will cause him/her to backwards over your extended leg. (See illustration Figure N.)

To be effective, however, *Lieh* must make use of the entire body, legs and waist as well as arms to "split" the attacker into two halves, moving in opposite directions. This is the symbolic image of heaven (upper body) separated and moving in conflict to the earth (lower body).

6. TUI (push)   trigram: TUI (marsh)

The essence of "pushing" an opponent away can be found in the act of breaking his/her connection with the earth. This is accomplished by moving straight into him/her and allowing his/her weight, and so his/her center of gravity, to be carried upon your own stance. Your attacker will momentarily feel as if he/she is walking upon soft, marshland soil. Once his/her connection to the ground is thus broken, the force of the attack may be easily redirected and translated into an upward projection. (See illustration Figure O.)

Place the palms of both hands upon both sides of his/her torso, somewhere near or below the floating ribs. Keep your elbows down near your own ribs and allow his/her forward pressure to slightly compress your weight into the ground through your rear foot. Now, shift your whole body along a downward arc onto your front foot. This should, if done properly, make you feel like a coiled spring. The elastic quality of your body's muscle tissues will allow you to effortlessly expand outward at about a forty-five degree upward angle, easily uprooting your opponent and propelling him/her backward at an alarming rate. You do not, however, "shove" him/her away from you. No, instead, your focus should be upon the downward and upward shift of your own body's center of gravity and weight.

7. DA (strike)   trigram: LI (fire)

Contrary to popular opinion, the fist is not a natural striking weapon. It is too easily damaged and requires far too much time and training to condition before it may be used as an adequate weapon. This does not meet with our definition of a "natural" weapon, one which is immediately usable and resistant to injury.

There are three primary striking weapons used in the art of *Tai-Yang Lung Tao*. First, and perhaps most important, is the heel of the open palm. Its inherent padding protects it from damage and, because it keeps the hand open, it can be instantly converted into a grab or a claw if the opportunity should present itself. Second, and perhaps most common, is the ridge-like side of the hand. This may be used either with a closed fist, acting somewhat like the head of a hammer, or with an open and tensed hand, delivered in a cutting or chopping motion. Third, and perhaps most powerful, is the bent elbow. It may be thrust upward into a hyperextended joint or the soft muscle tissue of an attacking limb, forward into the sternum or ribs, even backwards into the chest or abdomen of a person attacking from behind.

8. TI (kick)   trigram: CHEN (thunder)

Perhaps the most easily applied form of counterattack is a simple kick with the foot. Whenever an opponent steps into your *Chan-Su*, you could respond using a *Front Snap Kick* to the groin or lower abdomen with the ball of the foot. (See illustration Figure P-1.) Or, you could snap out a *Side Coil Kick* to the knee or shin with your out-turned heel. (See illustration Figure P-2.) Or, if you were to be attacked from behind, you could meet the assailant with a *Rear Stomp Kick* to his/her knee, shin or instep with either the heel or ball of your foot. (See illustration Figure P-3.)

However, no matter which kick you must utilize, it should be snapped out from a "chambered" position beside your knee and it should never be raised above the level of your own waist. Kicks to the head, which seem to be so popular in many martial arts, are not only unnatural but, quite possibly, self-damaging. When your leg is lifted above your own waist, you are top-heavy and rather off-balance. You also leave your groin and inner thigh open to attack. Besides, it could take years of stretching and strenuous practice before you become good enough to actually use such kicks with speed, power and accuracy. This would be of little consolation if you were to be assaulted tomorrow or next week. You need tools which are available to you right now.

With only these three kicks that lie hidden within the twisting steps of the DANCE OF THE SUN DRAGON, you may defend your lower extremities on a full three hundred sixty degree circle. The Front Snap Kick will cover an area of more than ninety degrees ahead of you. Left and right Side Coil Kicks will cover more than ninety degrees to either side. And, the Rear Stomp Kick will cover the final ninety degrees behind you. These overlapping quadrants will provide you with a full circle of protection.

Every martial arts technique has an infinite number of variations. We cannot, therefore, present in a single volume every possible application of these eight fundamental defensive characteristics. Even an entire series of books would still be inadequate to such a task.

As in all arts, the student must be able, at some point in the learning process, to make the miraculous leap from rote memorization to creative self-expression, and discover new variations never before revealed to him/her. In this type of educational development, not only is inventing new techniques possible, it is a requirement. Remember, however, that a good technique must be effortless, immediately effective, easy to learn, and possess a wide range of applicability.

Study carefully the many different forms of serpentine movements and defensive principles which they embody, and you will discover that no strike is unstoppable or any hold unbreakable.

RITUAL OF
CREATIVE VISUALIZATION

Everyone visualizes, whether it is merely in their dreams or as an effort of concentrated willpower. But, most people only channel the power of their psychic creativity into negative thoughts and materializations. They fear and worry about the future, dreading the worst and ignoring opportunities for betterment as they keep vigilant watch for an imminent disaster. Their own morbid expectations are a form of negative prayer, creating nervous tension (destructive force) in place of emotional intensity (creative power). Remember– be careful what you ask for in life, because you just might get it!!

Any form of self-limitation will shut the door upon the Spirit Self. For example: if you were to indicate a single specific source from which you expected your objective to arrive, you most probably would not see any results. What may have seemed the perfect and most obvious source of supply may not have been the right one for you. So, while you wasted your time chasing a fantasy, your real opportunity passed you unseen. It was not that your prayers went unanswered, but that you were too occupied with your own expectations to listen to the *Silent Voice* of your own God-Self.

Nothing is more uniquely intimate, after all, than the relationship between Deity and worshipper. But, for many it is almost impossible for them to imagine the Creator of All in any particular form, and even more difficult to visualize themselves in personal communication with their concept of Deity. That is why creative visualization is easier, in most cases, for the followers of a religion which has an overabundance of sacred images than it is for the followers of a more austere and imageless faith.

This does not, however, exclude the worshippers of an abstract God from receiving the benefits of prayer. They may simply substitute a great Spiritual Being (such as a saint or savior) for the image of God. This Spiritual Being, though, should not be mistaken for a god. He/She serves merely as a messenger to carry the worshipper's prayers to the Deity.

Here, in this manual, we shall use the image of the *Sun Dragon* as our spiritual messenger. But, if you are uncomfortable with this Chinese imagery, please feel free to substitute any image with which your heart and mind can identify. The nature of the messenger is not as important as the worshipper's own heartfelt sincerity.

Emergencies often prompt people to pray in sincerity who may never have prayed before. And, frequently, they will even receive that which they require of prayer. In such emergencies, a person has access to areas of the Deep Self which are normally kept hidden from the conscious mind, releasing an infinite ocean of pure Creative Power for the desperate personality to utilize in the achievement of its goal.

However, to pray effectively, without a real crisis, is something which you cannot count upon without concentrated practice. The path of devotion demands perseverance!!

Although it is not necessary to set up an elaborate ceremony, or even a special place, to perform your ritual of prayer, an altar and the proper furnishings will greatly augment your visualizations. If you can, obtain or make a small picture or sculpture in the likeness of your personal Deity or messenger. But, remember that you are not making a talisman, fetish or magical charm. This material image, in and of itself, has no real power. It is merely a symbol and, when your moment of worship is over, you must leave the stone or paper image upon the altar and put the True Image back within your heart.

Next, you will need to obtain a couple (2) of white candles, a small brass dish and incense of some subtle fragrance pleasing to you. These will be arranged around the image of *Tai-Yang Lung* (or whatever Divine Messenger you have chosen) on the little table of your altar. A black cloth should, first, be draped over the table. This, together with the white candles, is symbolic of the *Yin-Yang*, the dual polarities of the universe. The candles are, then, placed to either side of the Holy Image and the incense dish is set upon the table in front of the Sun Dragon.

The final piece of furniture needed to complete your altar is a small brass gong or bell and hammer. This will be placed on the floor, near where you will kneel to pray. You may also wish to place a pillow on the floor to comfort your knees. Be certain that the gong or bell is close enough to reach easily, without stretching, during your ritual.

These articles, the trappings of your altar, need not be possessions of the material world, however. Physical objects are but "things" and will be destroyed with the passage of time, but the possessions of the Spirit are eternal and cannot be polluted by mankind. If your altar and its furnishings are created upon the plane of thought, no one can ever steal them or destroy them, and you will be free of the restrictions of space. You may perform the *Ritual of the Sun Dragon* at any time and any place that you should find yourself. After all, the true ritual does not take place in the material realm at all. It is a ceremony of the Spirit merely reflected upon the physical world.

At one time or another, in the course of a lifetime, we all need to just get away from it all, to be alone with our own Inner Self. But, as our little planet becomes more and more crowded, it becomes harder and harder to find secluded spots which are within a practical distance of our homes.

And, it is impossible for most of us to simply run away to live on a mountaintop.

There is, however, one place which remains a private refuge for each and every one of us. That refuge is within the realm of the mind itself.

Before beginning your ritual, sit in a darkened room with your eyes closed and visualized the *Mountain Temple of the Sun Dragon*. This will be your sanctuary from the hustle and bustle of the material world. Here, you shall petition the Deity through the vehicle of *Tai-Yang Lung*, the Sun Dragon.

Since time out of mind, men/women have associated the highest peaks with the presence of the gods. Mount Sinai was the home of the Nameless God of Israel, and site of the Burning Bush through which God spoke to Moses. Olympus was the domicile of Zeus and the gods of Greek mythology. Even the austere Japanese revered Fujiyama (Mount Fuji) as the great steppingstone to the gods of their ancestors.

So, build your own mental sanctuary upon the top of a high mountain. It could be just a simple marble platform from which you may gaze out over the roof of the world, or an elaborately carved temple of jade, or a cathedral of gold and silver, ar any other structure which you can envision, as long as it is yours.

As with any other information presented throughout this book, this ritual of creative visualization is offered here only as a pattern or blueprint, which you may adopt or adapt to your personal needs and inclinations. If, however, you should decide to write your own ritual, we would urge you to follow the general guideline presented here.

Obviously, prayer may be initiated in any place and at any time necessary. But, traditionally, the *Ritual of the Sun Dragon* was performed during the Chinese hour of the dragon. This is a two hour period between seven o'clock and nine o'clock in the morning. If you wish to follow this tradition, we would suggest a time shortly before eight o'clock, at the peak of the dragon's power and vitality.

But, whatever time of day your ritual is performed, it should be at the same time each day. And, it should be performed only once per day until you objective is attained. To perform the ritual more than once a day would be like pouring water on a stone. Once it is wet, you will not make it any wetter by dousing it with more water. You will need to cultivate patience and allow time for the mechanism of life to operate, unhindered.

We would like to add a word of caution at this point, though. Do not, while performing these rituals, seek favor through any other psychic or spiritual means. This could weaken your confidence in your visualization and destroy the subtle connection with your own God-Self through the channel of your Divine Messenger. Be patient and allow your inner creative power time to bring your desire into materialization. You should, however, take any and all physical steps necessary to ensure success . . . without actually forcing the outcome!!

Begin your ritual by removing your altar furnishings from wherever they are safely kept, even if that is within your own mind. Spread the black cloth over the altar table and place the Divine Image of *Tai-Yang Lung* upon the altar with reverence. To either side of the Sun Dragon, place the white candles and light them. The brass incense dish is positioned before the Holy Messenger, filled and ignited. Finally, the lights should be completely extinguished, or the drapes drawn, so that the altar is illuminated by only the two candles.

Kneel before the altar, upon the cushion, close your eyes and visualize the Mountain Temple of *Tai-Yang Lung*. Feel the cool stone beneath you and the alpine breezes blowing across your skin. Create the image so strongly and clearly in the air about you that it is a reality, not just idle imagination.

Now, see a golden circle etched into the stones of the floor directly before you. It is in the shape of a blazing sun.

This is the *Sun Circle* into which you will project an image of your objective and charge it with your energies, a process known in Chinese as *Chi-Cheng* (concentration of *Chi*).

Formulate a clear idea of what it is you wish to achieve, and visualize it contained within the circle. It may be the healing of a family member who is ill or injured. It could be money which is needed to pay overdue bills. It may be a new job, a change of environment, or someone with whom to spend long quiet evenings. Anything and everything may be acquired in this manner. But, be careful what you ask for! If you need a hundred dollars, do not ask for a thousand. Your greed will taint the energies of your thought and set the wheels of *Karma* into motion, circling your own negativity through time and space to hit you in the back of the head, when you least expect it.

Strike the brass gong or bell three (3) times, and turn your inner sight to the sky above the temple. Visualize the great Dragon of Heaven descending from out of the fiery orb of the sun and coming to hover directly above you. See him/her clearly through the *Tien-Yen*, the third eye.

Bow low and speak words of sincere greeting to *Tai-Yang Lung* as he/she settles to the floor before you. Speak the words not just with your mouth but with your mind and heart as well, projecting the energies of your love and respect. Feel the blessed warmth of his/her love envelop you like a Divine Fire.

Visualize your objective enclosed within the golden ring of the Sun Circle. See it and yourself glow in the light of the Sun Dragon's fire. Do not take your eyes off this image as you begin to chant– "In the Divine Fire of the Sun Dragon I charge this image, that it may be realized for me in the material world. I petition *Tai-Yang Lung* to carry my humble request to the Creator of All That Is. Through the infinite love of the Dragon of Heaven may it be endowed with all the power of the Sun, Giver of All Life."

Look upward, through the *Tien-Yen* (the eye of heaven), and see *Tai-Yang Lung* depart, soaring into the blinding light of the sun. Bow your head and watch the glow of your objective slowly diminish within the Sun Circle as the great Dragon of Heaven delivers the energy of your thought to the Nameless God of All.

Strike the gong or bell three (3) times, bow low and make an act of heartfelt adoration to this Unseen One. Quietly and inwardly, chant–"Divine Parent, Creator of All, I ask the great Sun Dragon to carry this humble request to You on my behalf. May it be within Your will and the order of Destiny, please grant me this petition."

Now comes the hardest part of the entire ritual, the period of waiting. You must be very still and patient. Allow the great Dragon of Heaven time to commune with the Godhead. You must not attempt to call him/her back to the Earth, or you may destroy the fragile energies being brought together for your benefit.

When *Tai-Yang Lung* does return to the temple, you may hear his/her voice echoing across your mind, proclaiming that all will come to pass. But, if you should be told that your request has been denied, do not object or question the decision. There are always good reasons why certain prayers cannot be answered. It may be that you already have more than enough money and should not be asking for an additional supply. Or, perhaps, there are important spiritual lessons to be learned from the suffering of the present illness which could be learned in no other way.

Often, when a prayer cannot be answered, *Tai-Yang Lung* will suggest an alternate course of action. This is not just idle advice and should not be taken too lightly. But, if you insist upon your original proposal, be prepared to get exactly what you deserve–catastrophe!!

To conclude your ritual, strike the gong or bell three (3) more times and bow. As the image of the Sun Dragon fades back into the solar orb, and you return to the "real world," give thanks for the blessings bestowed upon you. Do not ever forget to express your gratitude. In fact, during the day or night, whenever you happen to recall *Tai-Yang Lung's* blessings, stop what you are doing and silently give thanks. You do not need to create another ritual or ceremony to express such sincere gratitude. Only a few seconds of silence are sufficient, if they are truly heartfelt.

Although the inner powers released through visualization and prayer may be utilized to obtain almost anything that the mind can imagine, they should never be used for "evil" purposes. You do create your own reality. Your every thought and deed are the tools with which you have built your world. If you choose to allow negative emotions to guide your actions, then your world will be one of extreme negativity and sorrow. But, follow the positive path and your world will be brighter and more alive.

However, even positive prayer can become destructive, if allowed to get out of control. Remember the story of the "Sorcerer's Apprentice" and his magic spell which ran wild? Any image which has been created for a good purpose, when no longer needed, will go out of control and harm its creator. But, the remedy is a simple one. When you objective has been attained, perform a special ritual in which you simply disintegrate its image and reabsorb the energy from the Sun Circle into yourself.

SOLITARY PATH INTO INFINITY

It was a foregone conclusion that this book would raise far more questions than it has feebly attempted to answer. But, regretfully, this was inevitable. No one book, or any one person, could possibly contain all the answers to all of life's endless questions. Perhaps that is exactly as it was intended to be, though.

Do not, for even a moment, think that your lessons have come to an end. Whether it is your first day of initiation into the martial arts or your seventy-first year of dedicated practice, you have but barely set you foot upon the path. There is still an infinity of principles, techniques and variations to be discovered within the simple framework of *Tai-Yang Lung Tao*. And we have had time to analyze but a few of these. The remainder are there, waiting for you to discover them for yourself as you explore the fathomless depths of your own unique form of individuality.

In the majority of Oriental traditions, there is no way that an individual can practice alone–membership in a "recognized" school is mandatory. Most of these traditional schools have a system with degrees of advancement, usually identified by various colored belts or sashes. Conformity to the system is a must for advancement and, with such a tradition, it is necessary for a student to progress to a certain degree before he/she is ever permitted to share his/her experiences through teaching. In order to test and promote other students, within the system, it is required that he/she attain the highest degree possible.

Such traditions are all well and good. Those involved in them seem quite content to follow the way of another, obediently and without question. But, it seems to us that an important point is being completely overlooked by such systems. Where is the opportunity for the expression of one's unique individual creativity. How is a person to find his/her niche in the grand procession of Life when he/she is merely imitating the movements and repeating the same empty words given to them by someone else.

No demonstration of techniques, words of explanation, or printed text will ever impart to you the wisdom and skill of the ancient "masters." The assimilation of such profound knowledge and awareness cannot be accomplished through osmosis. There simply are no such magical shortcuts to enlightenment.

Even the words and illustrations of this book are merely signposts, pointing the way. You alone must walk the path.

Do not let anyone tell you that, because you do not belong to any "legitimate" school or because you were not promoted by a certified master who was promoted by a master who was promoted by a master and so on, you are not a true martial artist. Schools and papers do not make one a martial artist. Even a high level of skill with your hands and feet will not make you a martial artist. To truly be a martial artist one must walk the path of the heart into the infinity of the Spirit. One must be a creator of peace in a world of violence. One must be a *Master of Life.*

GLOSSARY

One does not have to be Chinese to appreciate the wisdom of the ancient martial artists. It is unnecessary to become a part of their culture and speak their language. In fact, unless you are of Chinese ancestry, it is futile to try to become Chinese. Besides, how can you ever hope to discover your own individuality while you are pretending to be something you are not.

It is helpful, however, to understand a little bit about the Chinese terminology used within the martial arts. Single words can often convey much more than entire pages of text in the English language. It is, therefore, economy of time and energy that should motivate your study of this glossary, not a desire to create an air of mystery or historical mystique to your practice of *Tai-Yang Lung Tao.* An honest appreciation of the Chinese cultural traditions is natural and inevitable, due to the nature of the art itself. But, do not try to become Chinese.

AN	peaceful beatitude, a phase of meditation
CHAN-CHUANG	standing meditation
CHAN-SU	aura, literally "silk cocoon"
CHEN	thunder, trigram #8 of the I-Ching
CHI	"breath energy" of the inner emotional self
CHI	press down, third characteristic of defense
CHI-CHENG	concentration of Chi energy

CHING	release of thought, a phase of meditation
DA	strike, seventh characteristic of defense
DUNG-TAO	feeling as if the head is pulled upward on a cord
FA-JING	kinetic energy, emotional response as physical
FAN-CHAO	reflective awareness, result of meditation
FONG SU-YI	(1736-1820 AD) founder of Tai-Yang Lung Tao
FU-HSI	first emperor of China, author of the I-Ching
HSIANG-CHIAO BU	cross leg stance
HSU-JING	stillness within movement
HUN	conscious mind, fluctuation between Po and Shen
HUN-YUAN KUNG	natural posture
I-CHING	"Book of Changes" written by Fu-Hsi
JING	"seed energy" of the physical self, brute force
KARMA	retribution, law of cause and effect
KEN	mountain, trigram #2 of the I-Ching
KHAN	water, trigram #3 of the I-Ching
KUEN	pattern, plan or schematic of geometric design
KUMHWA	Korean village where Fong Su-Yi created his art

KUN	earth, trigram #1 of the I-Ching
KUNG-CHIEN BU	bow and arrow stance
KUNG-FU	effort and time spent in mastery of a skill
KWOU	throwing technique
LI	fire, trigram #7 of the I-Ching
LIANG-YI	the "Two Forms" or Yin-Yang essence of all things
LIEH	split fifth characteristic of defense
LIEN CHI HUA SHEN	transmuting physical force to spirit
LO	grabbing technique
LOK-MA	rooting of stance by sinking weight into earth
LU	roll back, second characteristic of defense
MA BU	horse stance
MAI-JIANG	elbows pressed inward and down against ribs
MANCHU	usurpers and rulers of China (1644-1912 AD)
MING	life-force of Jing, Chi and Shen combined
NI-CHAN	counterclockwise
NIEN	adhering or sticking to your opponent
OU	hooking technique
PA-KUA	the eight trigrams of the I-Ching
PA-MEN	"Eight Gates" or joints of the body
PENG	ward off, first characteristic of defense

PO	subconscious self
SAN-HO	the "Three Rivers" or energy centers
SAN-WEN	"Three Stabilities" or phases of meditation
SAN-YAO	the "Three Powers" of balance and harmony
SHAOLIN	monastery built near Teng-Fon-Hsien in Honan Prov.
SHEN	"Spirit energy" of the superconscious Self
SHUN-CHAN	clockwise
SU-HSIANG	the "Four Symbols" of earth, water, fire and air
SUN	wind, trigram #4 of the I-Ching
SUNG	to relax, a peculiar state of relaxed tension
TAI-CHI	the "Grand Ultimate" or Yin-Yang symbol
TAI-YANG	"Great Creative Energy," Chinese name for the sun
TAI-YANG LUNG	the Sun Dragon
TAN-TIEN	center of gravity and spiritual power
TAO	"The Way," spiritual path to oneness with nature
TI	kick, eighth characteristic of defense
TIEN	heaven, trigram #5 of the I-Ching
TIEN-YEN	"Eye of Heaven" or third eye of psychic sight
TING	fixation, a phase of meditation
TING-YU	complete vertical alignment of the spine
TO-NOA	a Complete Breath, literally "exhale-inhale"

TSAI	pull down, fourth characteristic of defense
TSOU	redirection, literally "lead by walking away"
TUI	push, sixth characteristic of defense
TUI	marsh, trigram #6 of the I-Ching
WU-CHI	"Void" or emptiness from which the universe came
WU-HUI	dance or rhythmic pattern of stepping and moving
WU-SHU	Chinese term for the martial arts
WU-TI	"no enemy - no rival"
WU-WEI	condition of "effortless effort"
YANG	positive polarity, male, aggressive, active, etc
YIN	negative polarity, female, receptive, passive, etc
YUAN	circular motion
YU-CHIA	Chinese yoga

Illustrations

YIN–YANG

Figure A.

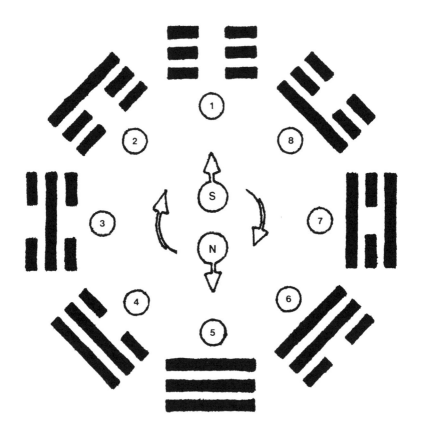

PA–KUA

Figure B.

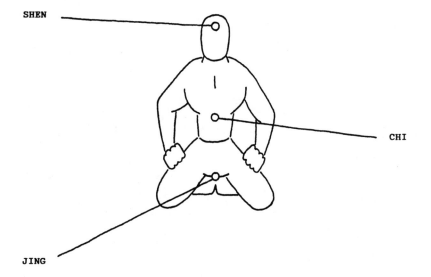

SHEN

CHI

JING

SAN–HO

Figure C.

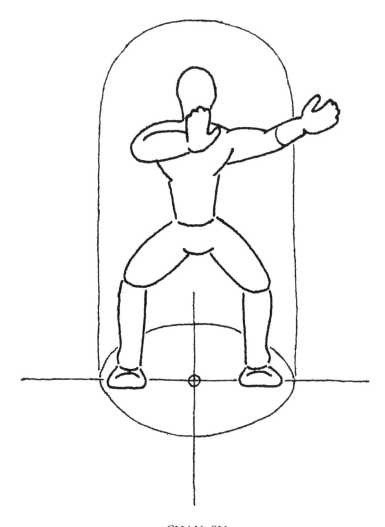

CHAN–SU

Figure D.

SERPENT RIDES WAVES

Figure E-1.

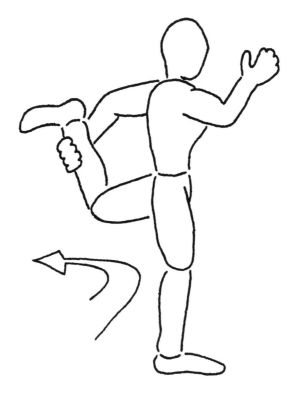

CRANE STRETCH

Figure E-2.

TEMPLE DANCER

Figure E-3.

SPEARMAN LUNGE

Figure E-4.

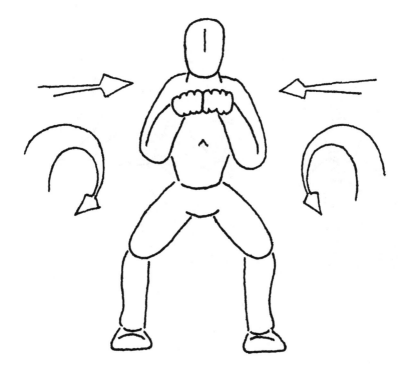

PULLING SILK

Figure E-5.

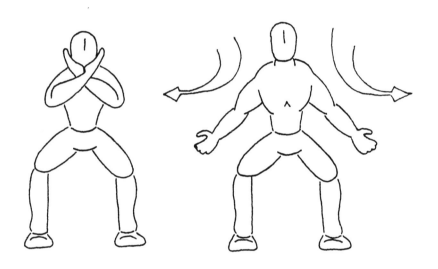

CRANE SPREADS WINGS

Figure E-6.

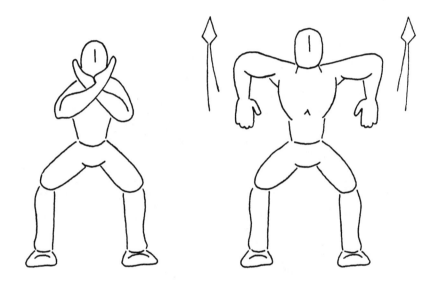

DRAGON LIFTS WINGS

Figure E-7.

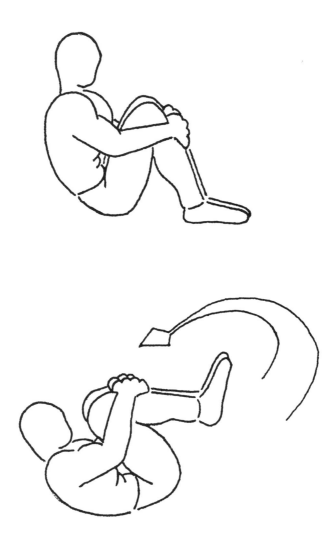

MONKEY ROLLS

Figure E-8.

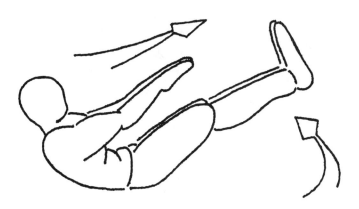

LOTUS REACHES TO SUN

Figure E-9.

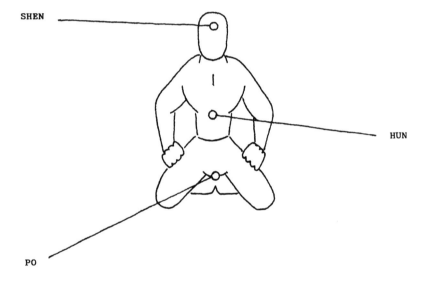

SAN–HO

Figure F.

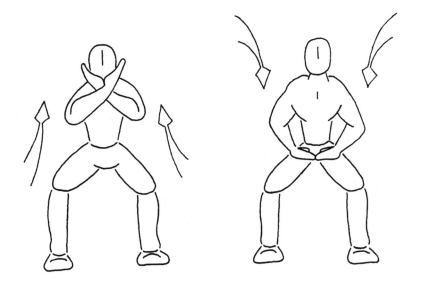

CIRCULATING THE LIGHT

Figure G-1.

ROTATING THE SPHERE

Figure G-2.

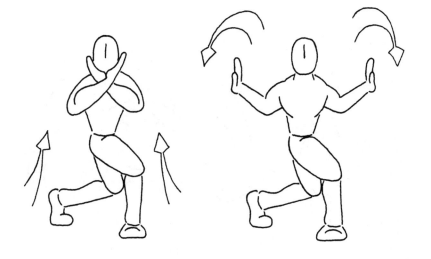

SPREADING THE LIGHT

Figure G-3.

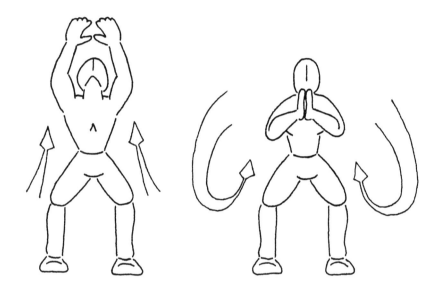

SALUTATION TO THE RISING SUN

Figure H-1.

DRAGON CIRCLES SUN

Figure H-2.

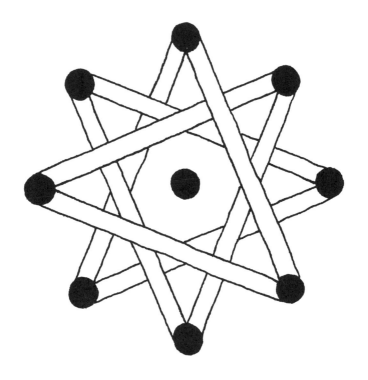

WU–HUI KUEN

Figure H-3.

DRAGON CIRCLES MOON

Figure H-4.

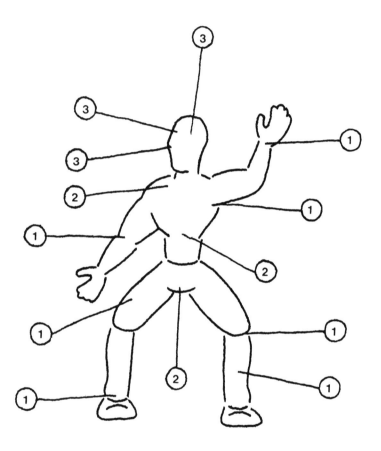

DEFENSIVE TARGETS

Figure I.

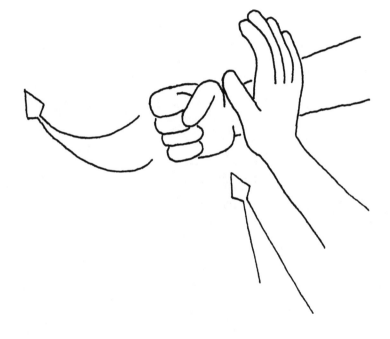

WARD OFF WITH PALM

Figure J-1.

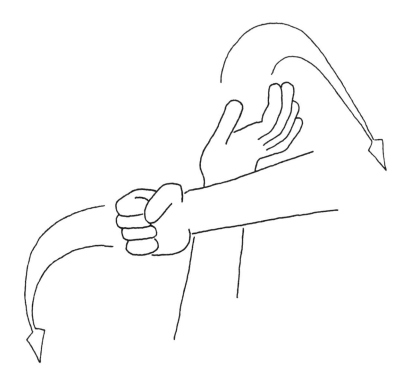

WARD OFF WITH HOOK

Figure J-2.

ROLL BACK

Figure K.

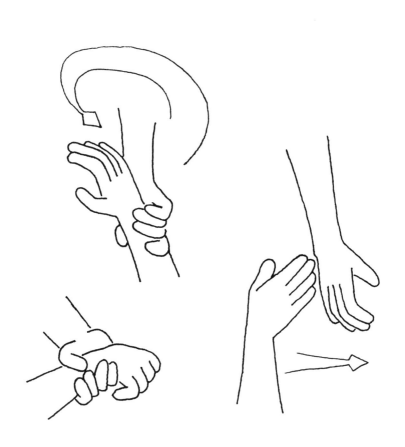

PRESS DOWN AND RELEASE

Figure L-1.

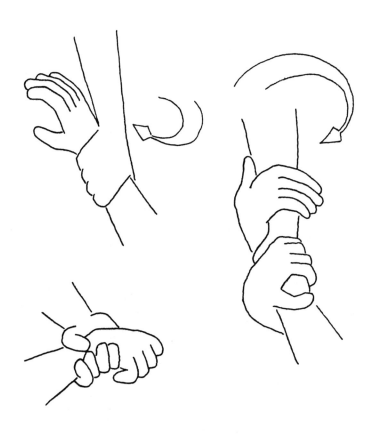

PRESS DOWN AND REVERSE

Figure L-2.

PULL DOWN AND NEUTRALIZE

Figure M-1.

PULL DOWN AND PROJECT

Figure M-2.

SPLIT

Figure N.

PUSH

Figure O.

FRONT SNAP KICK

Figure P-1.

SIDE COIL KICK

Figure P-2.

REAR STOMP KICK

Figure P-3.